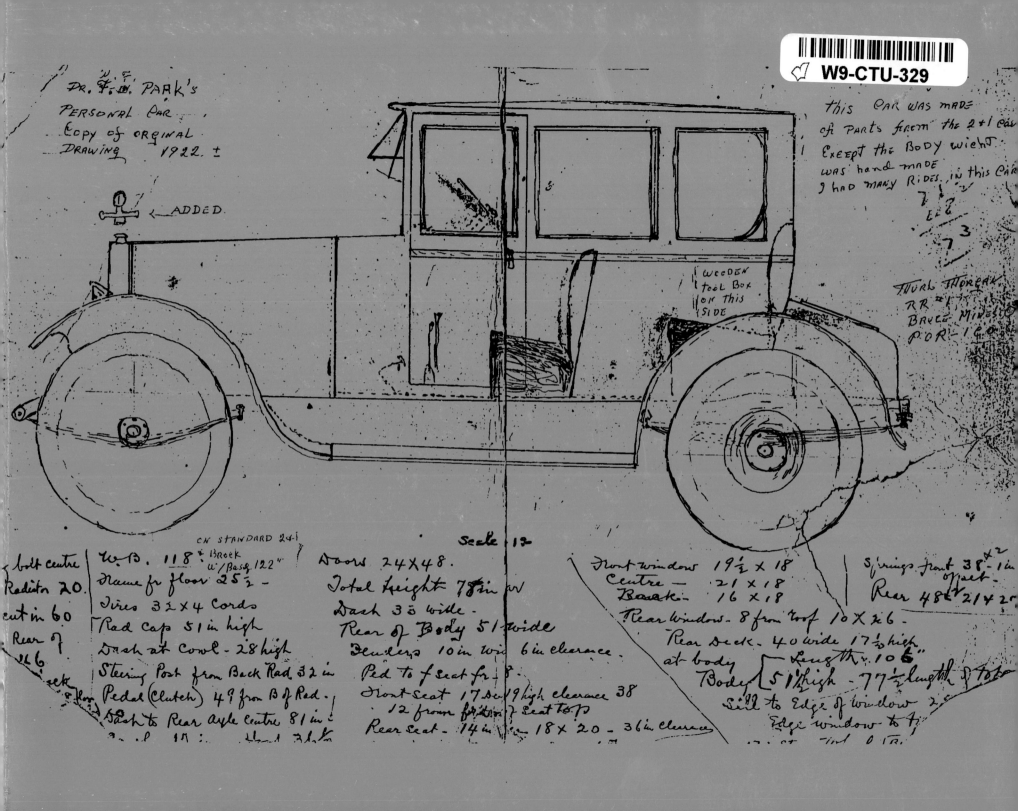

DR. F. W. PARK'S
PERSONAL CAR
COPY OF ORGINAL
DRAWING 1922. ±

← ADDED.

WOODEN
TOOL BOX
ON THIS
SIDE

this CAR WAS MADE
ofn PARTS from the 2+1 car
EXEPT the BODY wicht
WAS hand MADE
I HAD MANY RIDES in this CAR

THURL THOREAU
RR 21
BRUCE MINES
P.O.R. 160

CN STANDARD 24-1   Scale 1"

bolt centre   W.B. 118" Brock   Doors 24×48.   Front window 19½ × 18   Springs front 38
Raditor 20.   U/ Bash 122"   Total height 78in w   Centre — 21 × 18   offset
cut in 60   Name fr floor 25½ —   Dash 35 wide   Baaki 16 × 18   Rear 48 21 × 2
Rear of   Tires 32×4 Cords   Rear of Body 51 wide   Rear window- 8 from roof 10 × 26.
26   Rad cap 51 in high   Fenders 10in wid 6in clearance   Rear Deck. 40 wide 17½ high
seck   Dash at Cowl - 28 high   Ped to f seat fr. 8.   at body   Length 106"
floor   Steering Post from Back Rad 32 in   Front seat 17 dew 9 high clearance 38   Body 51 high - 77½ length of top
        Pedal (Clutch) 49 from B of Rad.   12 from fr seat top   Sill to Edge of window 2
        Dash to Rear axle centre 81 in   Rear seat - 14 in 18 × 20 - 36in clearance   Edge window to

PIONEERING THE AUTO AGE

by
Herb Colling
with
Carl Morgan

FORD OF CANADA ARCHIVES

COVER PHOTOGRAPH:

If a picture really is worth a thousand words, this one equals an entire chapter.

With a Ford truck prominent in the foreground and a horse and wagon almost lost in the background, the scene becomes a metaphor of the future.

Though many resisted change and clung to the "old" ways, by 1922, when this photo was taken at the Windsor train station, it was clear that motorized transportation had gained the high ground.

Canadian Cataloguing in Publication Data

Colling, Herb, 1953-
    Pioneering the auto age

Includes bibliographical references.
ISBN 1-895305-17-9

1. Automobile industry and trade — Ontario — Windsor — History. 2. Automobiles — Ontario — Windsor — History. I. Morgan, Carl II. Title.
HD9710.C23W46 1993   C93-090238-6
            338.4´76292´0971332

TraveLife Publishing Enterprises
12402 Riverside Drive East
Tecumseh, Ontario, Canada
N8N 1A3
Phone: (519) 735-6188   Fax: (519) 971-9675

Typesetting & Design: Benchmark Publishing & Design
                         1275 Walker Road
                         Windsor, Ontario, Canada
                         N8Y 4X9
                         Phone: (519) 971-9290
                         Fax: (519) 971-9675

Printed in Hong Kong

Contents

Dedication

We would be unspeakably remiss if we didn't extend a profound word of thanks and appreciation to our respective wives, Gloria Morgan and Anne Colling, for their unflagging patience through the long months we left them to their own devices as we burned the midnight oil to produce this book.

In those solitary times, if we weren't hunched over, staring glassy-eyed at a small dot skipping across our computer screens, we were fully engrossed, oblivious to almost everything else, as we searched for "one more" priceless photo, "one more" scrap of information, so necessary to breathe life into one of the most exciting periods of Windsor's history.

Without that total, enabling spousal support, *Pioneering The Auto Age* could never have been.

In the circumstances, it is unquestionably proper that this book be dedicated to Anne and Gloria for their cherished encouragement and support.

Acknowledgements

henever a book like this one — full of fascinating historical references and human anecdotes — makes its way to the market place — the question asked most often is:

"Where did you find all the information... the old pictures?"

The question is not easily answered. There simply is no single source, no mother lode, no magic device that spews everything out in tidy bundles.

The elements are out there, though. Somewhere.

Some are held in public libraries, museums, archives; others are preserved by private corporations... many are in prized, private collections. The trick is to find them. There's no substitute for plain, hard slogging, a lot of phone calls, a lot of door-knocking.

Even when the detective work is done, it would all be for nothing, without the unselfish co-operation of a lot of people.

We are deeply beholden to dozens of people who trusted us with their material with the simple understanding that, in due course, it would be returned in the same condition as it was borrowed.

We have tried very hard to justify that trust by producing the very best book possible... a unique book... one that tells much about the proud, 90-year history of the automotive industry of Windsor.

The following acknowledgements are not presented in order of importance. The last name is as important as the first.

Windsor Public Library: Erika Rebello, Senior Librarian; Lea J. Burton, Specialist, Science and Technology; Qiong Wu, assistant specialist; Brenda Main, Extension Services Librarian.

Ford Motor Company of Canada, Limited:

Dust goggles and other automotive memorabilia trigger memories from the early days of the automobile.

OAKVILLE: Tony Fredo, Vice-President, Public Affairs; Jim Hartford, Manager Public Affairs; Sandra Notarianni, Historical Consultant.

WINDSOR: Rick Poynter, Manager of the Employee Relations Department, Vera Grigorian, Section Supervisor, Salaried Personnel & Training, and Isabelle Higginbottom, Secretary in the Employee Relations Department; Charlie Edward, Employee Relations Associate, Training, Essex Engine Plant; Simon Ducharme, Area Manager, Windsor Engine Plant Number One; Donald Jones, Plant Engineering with the Windsor Casting Plant.

Chrysler Canada Limited, Windsor: Walter M.P. McCall, Manager of Corporate Public Relations.

General Motors:
OSHAWA: Stu Lowe, Manager External Relations.
WINDSOR: Paul Judd, Plant Manager, and Dan Garneau, Communications, Windsor Transmission Plant; Janis Bortolotti, Communications Co-ordinator, Windsor Trim Plant.

Staff members of the Canadian Auto Workers Union, Toronto: Jane Armstrong, National Representative for Public Relations, Toronto; and Tom Burton, Managing Editor of The Guardian of Windsor Inc., CAW Local 444, Windsor.

Georgia Klym-Skeates, Curator of the Transportation Museum and Heritage Village, Windsor Branch of the Historical Vehicle Society of Ontario.

The Hiram Walker Group: Gail Bost, Public Relations Co-ordinator; Percy Frith, Photographer; Jim Evans, former Community Relations Manager.

Windsor Truck and Storage: Fred Arthurs, Past-President, and Fred Baldwin, General Manage

The Windsor Star: Bill Bishop, Photo Editor; Bev MacKenzie, Photo Department Supervisor; Grant Black and Mike Weaver, Photographers; Deborah Jessop, Chief Librarian; Mike Ricketts and Ute Hertel, Library Assistants; Linda Balga, Manager, Community Relations Department

Windsor Police Services: Superintendent, Administration Division, John Burrows; Mary Jane McMullen, Assistant to the Planner.

Sheer happiness and exhilaration are mirrored on the faces of these "easy riders" as they experience the new-found freedom of the open road that came with the development of the automobile as a personal means of transportation.

Park House Museum, Amherstburg: Hazen Price, Treasurer; Valerie Buckie, Curator.

Tim and Denise Baxter, Flashbacks/Laser Prints.

Don Brown, Principal, Gordon McGregor Public School.

Evelyn Couch-Smith, Reporter, Essex Free Press, Essex.

Alan Douglas, retired Curator, Hiram Walker Historical Museum.

Ted Dudley, Model C Ford Owner, Pike Creek.

Mike Fairbairn, RM Auto Restoration, Chatham.

Tom Featherstone, Photo Archives, Wayne State University, Detroit.

Eleanor Gignac, Reporter, Amherstburg Echo, Amherstburg.

William Gregg, Military Vehicle Historian, Rockwood, Ontario.

David Guthrie, Chief of Visitor Activities, Fort Malden National Historic Site, Amherstburg.

Gerry Head, Librarian, CBC TV.

Phil Horner, Ford Security, retired, Windsor.

Bill Howitt, Historical Vehicle Collector, Windsor.

Peggy James, granddaughter of Dr. Fred Park, Amherstburg.

Roy Lancaster, retired President, Ambassador Bridge Corporation.

Judy Levesque, Registrar, Francois Baby House Museum

Walter McGregor, QC, nephew of Gordon M. McGregor, founder of the Ford Motor Company of Canada.

Joe Ouellette, Acrolab Instruments Ltd., Windsor.

Bob Paterson, Ford Inspector, retired, Windsor.

Lt. Col. Patrick J. Ryan, Essex Kent Scottish Regiment.

Nick Romanick, Historical Vehicle Collector, Windsor.

Leo St. Louis, Historical Memorabilia Collector, Windsor.

Jim Scratch, Historical Vehicle Collector, Windsor.

Gisele Seguin, Executive Director, Big Brothers Association.

Yvonne Sinasac, Artist, Amherstburg.

Mrs. Mary Speers, daughter-in-law of the late Charlie Speers.

Howard and Betty Watts, Historical Collectors, Brampton/Windsor.

George White, George White and Sons.

Elsie Wolf, former Executive Assistant and Recording Secretary to the Board of Directors, Transit Windsor.

Footnotes:

Because the dates of photographs and other illustrations appearing in this book were not always recorded at the time, many of the dates are approximations only.

The full name of the "François Baby House Museum" appearing in many credit lines is the "François Baby House: Windsor's Community Museum".

The names Ford Motor Company and Ford Motor Company of Canada, Limited are both correct and are used interchangeably.

The drawings of the Brock Six car that are used on the front and back end papers were generously made available by Mrs. Peggy James, of Amherstburg. She is the granddaughter of Dr. Fred Park, one-time mayor of Amherstburg. Dr. Park bought the parts, left over from the Two-in-One Car, and assembled the car himself. See Page 72.

The document at right is a copy of the original agreement between Henry Ford and Gordon Morton McGregor that gave birth to the Ford Motor Company of Canada.

AN AGREEMENT made and entered into at the City of Detroit, Michigan, U.S.A. this tenth day of August, A.D., 1904

BETWEEN:

FORD MOTOR COMPANY of Detroit, Michigan, U.S.A. (Hereinafter called the Michigan Company)

of the First Part

GORDON M. McGREGOR of the Town of Walkerville, in the County of Essex, Ontario, Manager,

of the Second Part,

—and—

HENRY FORD, of the City of Detroit, Michigan, U.S.A., Inventor,

of the Third Part

WHEREAS the Michigan Company aforesaid (a Company incorporated under the laws of the State of Michigan) is engaged in the manufacture of automobiles at Detroit, aforesaid, and in connection with its business is the owner of certain patents of invention for the construction of automobiles

AND WHEREAS, the said Michigan Company have certain patents, patterns, models, plans, drawings, specifications, machinery, tools and appliances which have in connection with the mechanical ingenuity of Henry Ford, party of the third part herein, been found to be and are of great commercial value as applied to the construction of Automobiles and is desirous of widening the field of their application in the interests of its stockholders and of promoting the objects of this Agreement, which have been duly submitted to them,

AND WHEREAS the said party of the second part in this Agreement represents the owners of a certain piece of real estate in the Township of Sandwich East, in the County of Essex, and buildings, engines, boilers, dynamo and electrical fixtures thereon at present used and occupied by the Walkerville Wagon Works, Limited, and also represents certain cash subscribers for stock in a proposed Canadian Company to be known as the Ford Motor Company of Canada, Limited, to be incorporated with a Capital Stock of $125,000.00,

AND WHEREAS the said Gordon M. McGregor and those whom he represents are desirous of forming a Canadian Automobile Company,

NOW, THIS AGREEMENT WITNESSETH, that in consideration of the premises and of One Dollar of lawful money of the United States of America now paid by the

In The Beginning

FORD OF CANADA ARCHIVES

The first Canadian Ford, 1904 — Model C.

A t the turn of the century Windsor began life with the auto industry, enduring both the pain and joy of birth... the years of discovery and experimentation... the uncertainty of adolescence.

In the grey Dawn of the Automotive Age, Windsor's future was no more promising than her past. That changed dramatically when a few enterprising businessmen enticed the Ford Motor Company, then in Flint, Michigan, to cross the border and sink new roots in a small town called Walkerville.

Few people realized the importance of the car and the impact it would have on everyone, everywhere, in the years ahead. In that respect, Windsor and a clutch of remarkable visionaries were on the cutting edge of a new age.

Windsor has been home to more car and truck manufacturers *than any other city* in the Dominion, churning out an astonishing array of vehicles to meet a variety of needs.

There is little question that Windsor put Canada on wheels.

Many of the car and truck companies that sprang up throughout the city are still household names... Ford, Studebaker, Packard, Dodge, Chrysler, McLaughlin-Buick, Hupmobile. Others are little more than faint memories of another era. How many still remember Menard, Gramm, Reo, Gotfredson or Tate?

There were no guarantees, no warranties, for the people who gambled on a dream. Fortunes were made and lost in a real-life game of winner-take-all. Some companies lasted decades, others a few years. Some never got off the ground. At the end of the day, though, they all contributed to the colourful industrial mosaic of this community.

As the intense competition took its toll, smaller companies vanished or were absorbed, until only the Big Three remained. From the mid-1920s, Windsor has been the *ONLY* Canadian city able to boast the presence of GM, Ford and Chrysler — giving added credence to the city's reputation as the Automotive Capital of Canada.

That's only part of the story.

Less well known is Windsor's incredible automotive contribution to the Allied forces during World War Two. It's a matter of record that Canada produced more military machines than any other country in the British Empire — and most of them came from Windsor!

Ford Motor Company was Canada's leading manufacturer of military vehicles during World War Two. By war's end, it had produced 28,988 Universal Carriers (above). See Pages 81-90.

Horse-drawn trolleys like this one were in use by the Amherstburg, Windsor and Sandwich Railway long before motorized buses were available. SW&A eventually bought a fleet of made-in-Windsor Ford buses. See Page 28.

The stories that follow in these pages offer a glimpse of that passing parade... from the earliest days, when Windsor dominated the car-building scene, to the more recent emergence of parts manufacturing, tool-and-die and mold-making industries — all crucial to the car-making business.

Pioneering the Auto Age is more than a story of metal, machines, and motors — it is the classic story of the defiant, determined, resilient people who made it all happen.

Once again, it is the stuff of history.

Part One:
The Years Of Discovery

Think of this:
Purely and simply, the Canadian car and truck industry was born and raised in Windsor!
The Ford Motor Company put Windsor on wheels, and Windsor put Canada on wheels!

The Auto Age Changed Everything, Forever

A mericans developed the assembly line and perfected mass production, but the French coined the word "automobile" from the Greek "self" and the Latin "moving" — a term adopted throughout the world.

Although interest in self-powered vehicles spread rapidly, the automobile's penetration of North America wasn't an overnight journey — it was more of a gradual but relentless shuffle into the most isolated corners of the land.

The first sighting of an automobile in Essex County was on July 6, 1900, in North Ridge a hamlet southeast of Windsor. The second was on Friday, August 24, in Kingsville, on the shores of Lake Erie. A newspaper reported:

"An automobile from Detroit struck town on Tuesday and created quite a sensation."

Two more entered Ruthven in October.

"A happy crowd heading for Niagara Falls."

Cars caused a stir wherever they went. At Sarnia, customs officers didn't know how to classify the first car, so they called it farm machinery.

In 1901 Roy D. Chapin, sales manager for Oldsmobile, finally talked the captain of a ferry into letting him board with his machine. Chapin was heading for a New York auto show, but, before heading east, drove around Windsor so he could say the car was "internationally tested."

Although interest in the automobile was growing, this was still a horse-and-buggy society and the transition was difficult. The infernal machines were seen by many as a nuisance. Foes included the Women's Institute of Ontario, a politically powerful rural organization which crusaded against autos, fearing that attendance at meetings would drop because of the danger of cars on the streets.

BAXTER/LASER PRINTS

Before the arrival of the automobile, streets and roads in town and country were rough, rutted and unpaved.

Early automobiles head down Ferry Hill at the foot of Ouellette Avenue to meet the incoming steam ferries which would then take them to Detroit.

The Age of the Automobile opened many doors of opportunity that simply did not previously exist. Sales calls and delivery of goods to rural general stores became a matter of course. This 1920s scene shows a 1919 Model T Roadster and an early Ford truck.

One report from Amherstburg said the auto kept farmers' wives and daughters off the road. One woman complained:

"Why should the people who cleared the land and built the roads have to abandon them to the rich man and his automobile?!"

A Sarnia judge banned a car from the streets, citing it as a danger because it caused a horse to bolt, upsetting a buggy and injuring a passenger. In one incident, a horse reared, and ripped a hoof through the car's hood. The buggy driver reckoned the animal showed remarkable horse sense.

Another horse dropped dead from fright so farmers began pasturing their colts beside the roadways, to get them used to cars. That incident might also have prompted this Essex County bylaw:

"If your horse is afraid to face an automobile on the road, hold up your hand and the driver of the motor vehicle must stop and assist you to pass."

Travelling was hazardous, especially during the winter when roads were slick with ice and mud. Cars offered speed and distance, but they often broke down and garages were scarce.

Horse racing was legal in Ontario but not in Michigan. On race days, dozens of cars came over by ferry and paraded up Ouellette Avenue to the Jockey Club (Jackson Park), or to the

This sporty looking 1909 Ford Touring car was the cover photo of the 1974 edition of Vintage Canada, *published by the National Association of Antique Auto Clubs of Canada.*

TED DUDLEY COLLECTION

Kenilworth or Devonshire tracks, roughly where Devonshire Mall and the Roundhouse Centre now stand.

Motorists paid a licence fee and bought a marker to drive legally in Ontario. Speed was limited to ten miles an hour in town and 15 in the county. By mid-summer, 1910, nine Detroit drivers paid fines totalling $130 for travelling five miles over the limit.

World War One catapulted Canada — and Windsor — into the industrial limelight. This country produced 150,000 trucks and other specialized military vehicles including staff cars and ambulances. Canada became the number two producer of motorized vehicles behind the U.S., a position it held until 1923.

At the turn of the century, 15,000 people lived near Windsor. European, with a strong work ethic, they were skilled with carriages and boats; on farms and in sawmills — a ready, reliable workforce. Fifteen years later, there were twice as many people; 1,500 worked for Ford.

The Evening Record extolled Windsor's virtues as a manufacturing centre. The city was close to iron ore and coal deposits in Michigan and Pennsylvania. There was good rail and water transportation and ample power supplies. Windsor's proximity to Detroit was also a major factor in the industry's development. Since Canada enjoyed preferential trade with the British Empire, it made sense for Americans to open branch plants on this side of the border.

The mushrooming growth of the industry inspired *The Record* to comment that "money is plentiful and business and manufacturing conditions are in good shape because of the war. There are four truck firms: Gramm, Menard, The Canadian Commercial Motor Car Company and New Dominion Motors; and 21 parts supply companies making headlights, trim, bodies and wheels. Steel works and foundries are also in production to accommodate the new industry."

At war's end, traffic increased and there was a need for better roads. Work started on a highway linking Windsor to Montreal and a system of provincial grants was introduced. It was aptly named the Good Roads Movement and Essex County was among the first in Ontario to become involved.

The Windsor Police Department was one of the first motorized forces in the country, beginning with a Harley

Perhaps it was because Windsor was quickly recognized as the Automotive Capital of Canada; perhaps it was because of the city's proximity to the American border; perhaps it was because of the need to keep ahead of the rum-runners, but the Windsor Police Department was one of the first motorized forces in the country. It acquired a Harley Davidson motorcycle in 1917. Then, to match the rum-runners, bought its first car. The rum-runners named theirs the "Whiskey Six;" police preferred "The Flyer".

Davidson motorcycle purchased in 1917. Then, to keep up with rum-runners in the Roaring 20s, the force bought its first car.

In 1920 the Border Cities Auto Show was held for the first time at the Windsor Armouries. It was the largest show of its kind in Canada, promoting the area as an industrial community where the automobile was king. The next year the show lasted all week, featuring musical programs, cars, trucks, tractors and even bicycles. More than 15,000 attended, rivalling the Detroit show which started in 1902.

By 1922, Essex County had 8,000 cars and, on a population basis, boasted more pavement than any other county in the country. Talbot, Middle and Front roads were paved and regular bus service ran between Windsor and Harrow.

If the automobile provided new freedom for owners, it also created new problems for police. Cyclists, enjoying one of the most popular pastimes of the day, were often clipped or

forced off the road. Children ran into the paths of cars, prompting Chief Constable Daniel Thompson to warn parents of the dangers.

In 1923, stop signs were posted at major intersections and within a year, accidents dropped from 468 to 267 — still high considering the few cars on the streets.

Two years later, Windsor became the first city of its size to install a street light. It cost $8,000 and did the work of four officers. People weren't happy, though. They missed the "big policeman" who helped their children cross the street. They didn't understand the red, green and amber lights and the system didn't help at night because it was turned off.

Parking tickets or "cards" were introduced in 1926 and the city collected almost $2,000 in fines. Chief Constable Thompson reported that, as a courtesy, he issued warnings to visitors.

Parking problems increased as Ouellette Avenue matured. Businessmen were urged to park in garages, leaving streets open to their customers — a problem that still exists today.

Windsor's ties with Detroit and its burgeoning auto industry caused a tremendous increase in cross-border traffic. Car ferries carried only 75 vehicles causing long lines at the docks. Overnight delays were common on weekends and holidays.

Two solutions evolved almost simultaneously — constuction of the international bridge and tunnel.

On November 11, 1929, the Ambassador Bridge opened. Thousands attending the ceremonies couldn't be controlled as they crashed the barricades, swarming onto the new structure. It signalled the beginning of the end for the ferries that had served commuters for a century.

A year later, a parade opened the Detroit-Canada Tunnel on November 3, 1930, at a cost of $25,000,000. This first international underwater subway moved 2,400 cars an hour.

The euphoria was short-lived, however, as the auto industry faced the economic onslaught of the Great Depression. Manufacturers absorbed punishing blows, but, for the survivors, there was tremendous prosperity as the car emerged as a major part of North America's social and economic fabric.

The auto industry brought a sense of unaccustomed pride to the city, and boosted a sluggish economy. People earned good money — and they spent it. Photo at right puts this new-found prosperity into perspective. Fresh opportunities were the order of the day as there was money available for new cars and classy duds for the Uptown Swells.

An artist's conception illustrates the three methods of transportation across the Detroit River. Opening of the Ambassador Bridge and Detroit-Canada Tunnel rang down the curtain on the old steam ferries which had provided this service for decades.

Automotive "Pioneers" Had Uncommonly Inquisitive Minds

Call them tinkerers, call them inventors, call them pioneers. They were men with uncommonly inquisitive minds who set their own rules and marched to their own drum-beats. They cared little for fame or fortune, and spent their waking hours more obsessed with making things work than keeping records of what they did.

There are few clues to tell us when the automobile made its debut, chugging and wheezing along the rutted backroads of 19th Century Canada.

One early reference is to a self-propelled Canadian steam buggy built by Henry Seth Taylor, a goldsmith and jeweller from Stanstead, Que. It was 1867 — the year Canada became a nation.

Locally, the desire to build a carriage powered by anything but horses teased the imagination of William Bulmer, an inventor and jack-of-all-trades. Bulmer was born in Sandwich, now Windsor's west end. His parents were teachers and their legacy to him was a fertile imagination.

This soft-spoken, skillful man worked alternately as a carpenter and plumber. He invented an efficient gas burner, and was an undertaker who built his own hearse and also ran a furniture factory in Sandwich. He invented a scald-proof kettle and earned his Ship Master's Certificate, qualifying him to serve as a riverboat captain. He survived two marriages and fathered 10 children.

In 1886, Bulmer built a steam yacht for a man from Jackson, Michigan. He later adapted his knowledge of marine engines to power a land vehicle. Within six months, he built a steam carriage in his shop next to McKinney's Meat Market at 75 London Street West — now University Avenue. His buggy cost $700 and sported iron tires and 340 feet of copper tubing connected to a 50-pound marine engine and a boiler bolted under the two-passenger seat. It carried enough fuel to heat 18 gallons of water.

This three-wheeled, steam-powered, coke-burning automobile was built in Bouton, France, and is one of the oldest self-propelled machines in existence.

Bulmer boasted that his horseless carriage could get up steam in five minutes, had a range of 100 miles and could chug along at 20 miles an hour.

A friend offered to invest $2,000 so Bulmer could manufacture the car commercially, but the inventor declined. He built the first one for the fun of it, and calculated that he'd have to build too many to recover his costs. Besides, factory-built vehicles were becoming more plentiful, popular, reliable and cheap.

Bulmer, a 19th Century tinkerer and inventor — a man with a restless mind — was one of the uncounted, driven pioneers who laid the groundwork for the auto industry in Canada.

In the 1950s, when Bulmer was well into his 80s, he admitted he never dreamed the day would come when almost everyone owned a car.

The photograph at right is one of the earliest known to exist showing the interior of the Ford Motor Company plant in Windsor. It was taken about 1904-05.

Windsor: Birthplace Of Canada's Car And Truck Industry

No other city can claim the distinction of being the birthplace of Canada's car and truck industry!

On August 17, 1904, the Ford Motor Company of Canada, Limited was born in Windsor — and, while not the first car company to take root in this country, it is the oldest of the pioneers with a continuous, uninterrupted presence.

Credit goes to Gordon Morton McGregor, manager-owner of Walkerville Wagon Works overlooking the Detroit River near the foot of Drouillard Road. At 31, McGregor inherited the carriage works when his father died. The company was losing money and, at the urging of John Curry, his banker, McGregor sold everything but the factory building. He was without a job and $75,000 in debt.

McGregor was confident that people wanted cars and figured he was the guy to build them. Rather than start from scratch, he allied himself with someone already in the business. He called Curry and, with a group of businessmen, headed to Detroit.

Gordon McGregor

Computers, lasers and other 20th century, state-of-the-art electronic gadgetry measure, with unimaginable precision, every component that goes into the manufacture of today's automobiles. In earlier days, visual inspections were carried out by workers such as this man checking the crankshaft of a Model A.

They first met Henry Martin Leland at the Cadillac Automobile Company, then arranged a meeting with a struggling inventor named Henry Ford.

Ford, a mechanical whiz, built his first steam engine when he was 15. In 1896, he designed and built his first quadricycle while working as an engineer with the Edison Illuminating Company.

Ford liked people with bright ideas and listened to McGregor's pitch. It was a historic meeting — giving birth to the Ford Motor Company of Canada Limited.

McGregor got the rights to sell the Ford automobile in Canada and the British Empire, except the British Isles, which Ford kept for himself. McGregor also received all Canadian patents, plans, drawings and specs and the right to operate independently from his American counterpart. The payback for Ford was easy access to Canada and the British Empire.

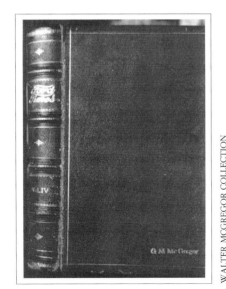

Leather-bound edition of 1911 Ford Times magazines is stamped in gold with the name of Gordon M. McGregor, founder of Ford of Canada.

Pioneering The Auto Age

Right: Each shift change saw thousands of workers pouring into and out of the mammoth Ford plant on Riverside Drive near Drouillard Road.

Below: A streetcar took workers directly to and from the plant gates.

McGregor had to raise $125,000, no easy task since most investors still saw the auto business as a high-risk gamble. Canadians were particularly wary because Ford's company was only seven months old and he had two previous failures. In the end, most of McGregor's money came from Michigan. Only $55,000 was from Canadian sources including Charles and John Stodgell; Robert Gray, who was in the car business in Chatham; and Wallace R. Campbell, who began as a bookkeeper, but eventually became the company's first Windsor-born president.

Curiously, McGregor never became president of the firm he founded. He was the secretary and general manager until his death in 1922. Initially, he was also in charge of sales, since there were only three people in the office. Besides McGregor and Campbell, there was Grace E. Falconer, the only woman

The Years Of Discovery

WINDSOR STAR LIBRARY

WINDSOR STAR LIBRARY

For years, the huge Ford complex was one of the most important mainstays in Windsor's industrial economy. The aerial photo (above) shows the sprawling operation before 1951 when the company announced it would shift the assembly plant to Oakville. Demolition crews converted the structure to a pile of rubble (left).

on staff. She started as a stenographer and became private secretary to the president, spending over 40 years with Ford.

The U.S. parent company, with 51 per cent of the shares, appointed nine directors, mostly Michigan stock holders. The first president was John F. Gray, then head of the American firm and second largest stockholder. Ford became a paid advisor and vice-president. Curry was treasurer.

During the first five years, some investors lost confidence and sold their stock for 75 cents on the dollar. Those who held on, made a fortune. McGregor cleared his debt and his new firm paid substantial dividends by 1909. The Stodgells, who bought five shares for $500, sold them during the Depression for $10,000.

Home for Ford of Canada was the former Walkerville Wagon Works — a brick, two-storey building with a loft, blacksmith shop, power-house, three metal-clad warehouses and several smaller buildings.

Assembly was on the ground floor of the main building, while the painting of the body, chassis and wheels was on the second floor. The assembly room floor was thick with paint drippings, the walls splotched with colour. The only power machinery were a drill press and a freight hoist, driven by a belt running from the rear wheel of a Model C Ford!

The Canadian plant started too late to produce the original Model A, so it began with the B and C. It was a struggle, but McGregor assembled cars one-by-one with chassis and other parts ferried from Detroit, then relayed by horse and wagon to the factory. Wrong parts were often shipped or lost, forcing McGregor to lose time.

Despite the hardships, 17 employees cheered in October, 1904, when McGregor drove the first Model C down Sandwich Street. It was a light-weight, two-cylinder car with a fake hood, an engine under the seat and top speed of 30 miles an hour. It was an open-top, high-riding contraption well deserving of the name, horseless carriage. It sold for $1,100.

Henry Ford

Ted Dudley smiles happily behind the wheel of his 1905 Model C, one of the first cars built in the fall of 1904 at the Windsor Ford plant. At one time he raced it at Greenfield Village, Dearborn, Mich. Rules required the drivers to crank the engines, climb into the driver's seat, and head for the finish line, a couple of hundred yards distant.

The company produced 110 model C's and seven Model B's the first year. The B was a larger, four-cylinder car with a real hood. The Ford payroll was $12,000 including $2,400 for Ford and $2,000 for McGregor.

In 1906, Ford became president of the Canadian firm, a post he held for 21 years.

George Dixon, a tool-maker for the firm in those days, remembered Ford spending hours in the Canadian plant, explaining it to his son, Edsel. Dixon earned the incredibly high wage of 35 cents an hour because of his skill making front axles. The average worker made 17 cents, at a time when a good meal with a beer cost 20 cents and a hotel room cost $12 a month.

1917: The rapid development of the automobile was big news when this movie crew came to town and produced a "newsreel" about Ford that was shown in movie houses everywhere.

The winged Ford emblem shown at right was proudly displayed throughout the Ford Motor company empire in the 1920s and '30s. It was even prominent over the main entrance of the Post Office of Ford City.

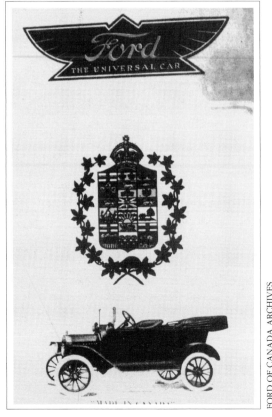

Exports outnumbered domestic sales three-to-one and the company was shipping as far as India and New Zealand. Subsidiaries were set up in those countries by the Canadian firm and those overseas operations sometimes kept Ford in the black when home sales were down.

A Canadian dealer network was also being established, with one dealership run by Gordon's brother, W. Donald McGregor.

Sandwich Street was used as the Ford test track for new cars. Production of a dozen cars a week was cause for celebration and they presented quite a sight, huffing and puffing along dusty summer streets or through the mud and slush of winter at 15 miles an hour.

Across the street was the Dew Drop Inn, a hotel where Ford workers spent their half-hour lunch, sometimes joined by McGregor. The specialty was fish, usually pickerel, freshly caught from the Ford plant docks. Some workers spent their break swimming in the Detroit River.

Workers walked or rode their bikes to work on the dirt streets and the wood sidewalk in summer, or on the streetcar tracks that were cleared in the winter. When Our Lady of the Rosary Church at the foot of Drouillard Road caught fire, Ford workers were there to help fight it.

In 1907, production tripled to 327 cars, thanks to the addition of the fancier R and S models. The next year, Ford produced 486 vehicles and was about to make automotive history with mass production and the new Model T. One hundred and fifty workers produced 18 Model T's in a 10-hour day.

Ford of Canada was on a roll and, by 1910, had outgrown the old wagon works. In its first major expansion, the company built a three-storey building, adding 200,000 square feet. Output soared to 1,200 units — a fantastic increase. The following year, 6,500 cars were produced by 1,000 workers. Ford staff increased to 2,000 in 1915 and 5,300 by 1924 — with corresponding increases in production.

In 1911, a more efficient, four-storey concrete building opened with almost 20,000 square feet. A second building followed a year later with twice the space. Ford was the largest automobile manufacturer in the British Empire.

A Windsor-built Ford was the first car in Turkey and there were Fords on the streets of Barbados, Kuala Lumpur, Japan, China, South Africa and India. Ford had distribution centres in nine Canadian cities. The only car dealership in Newfoundland was Ford.

The old wagon works came down in 1912, making way for the company's first office building. A year later, Ford produced its own engines in Windsor.

As more roads were paved, McGregor opened his first manufacturing plant on property in Sandwich East Township, abutting Walkerville. The village that grew up around the factory was incorporated as "Ford City" in 1913, though the company referred to it as "Ford, Ontario" and carried that name on all company stationery.

It became a town in 1915, boasting its own post office with the familiar, winged Ford emblem over the door. The name, Ford City, was a misnomer as it never did reach city status. It was changed to East Windsor in 1929 and that name disappeared following annexation by Windsor in 1935.

With the onset of mass production, Ford developed an unexpected problem in the paint department. Cars were painted with a primer coat, followed by one or two layers of flat colour topped with varnish. It did a fine job, but was far too slow to keep up with the more sophisticated, moving assembly line.

Ford switched to a fast-drying black enamel previously reserved for the wheels. From 1914 to 1925, "Japan Black" was the colour of choice, although Ford of Canada offered dark blue in 1915 and blue-green from 1916 to 1918. After that, Canada adopted Henry Ford's half-humourous policy that you could have "any colour you wanted as long as it was black."

When World War One broke out, Ford turned out hundreds of military cars, trucks and ambulances. In 1914, it even produced a car equipped with a machine gun. In 1917, Ford set a Canadian record of 50,000 vehicles.

1926: Direct access to road, rail and water transportation made Windsor an ideal location for Ford, which shipped cars and trucks across Canada and around the globe.

It was a proud day when Ford turned out its one-millionth car. At left is Wallace Campbell, first Canadian-born president of the company. At right is George Dickert, Ford of Canada superintendent.

1915: When this photo was taken, 2,000 workers were employed at the Ford plant. To take this picture with the least amount of work disruption, the photographer arranged his equipment before the workers were called out.

FORD OF CANADA ARCHIVES

In 1922, Ford spent $2,000,000 and opened its sprawling Plant Two, the biggest expansion to that time. The plant was so large that the men quipped, "give us a map of the place so we can get home for supper." That year, 70 per cent of all cars sold in Canada were Windsor-built Fords.

Ford City police bought a Ford touring car. Until then they hired drivers or took prisoners to jail by taxi. Their new vehicle was equipped with an extra tire, a speedometer, and spotlight.

In 1926, the Ford plant closed for a year to complete a major retooling to launch the new Model A — the most talked about automotive event of the year. It was 40 horsepower, with a four-cylinder engine.

Wallace Campbell

Meantime, things were looking bright for Wallace R, Campbell, the man hired as a bookkeeper in 1904 at the tender age of 23. By 1929, he became the company's first Canadian president, succeeding Edsel Ford who had taken over in 1927. Campbell served until 1946 and was the first in an unbroken succession of Canadians to hold the top job.

By 1931, Ford had produced more than 1,000,000 cars and was about to introduce its new V-8 engine which became the basic Ford engine for the next 22 years.

During World War Two, Ford employees voted to join the United Auto Workers Union. The vote was supervised by the federal government on November 13, 1941. Ford, one of

Rhys Sale

TED DUDLEY COLLECTION

"Trading up" is not an activity unique to contemporary car buyers — it was a practice that caught on in the early days as automotive engineers were jazzing up their designs with full sides, fixed tops, windows and attractive paint jobs.

until 1960. During his term, the Windsor assembly line was phased out. The news, on October 31, 1951 shook the area. It was hard to believe that Ford of Canada, born and nurtured in Windsor, would shift its entire car and truck assembly to Oakville.

Ford's administration, with the exception of its export operation, also moved. By 1954, it was the end of the line for Ford assembly in Windsor. Thousands of Ford employees and their families mourned the loss as they worked to put their lives in order. Some transferred to the Niagara Falls glass plant, 350 went to Oakville. Others joined the lines of the unemployed.

To placate the union, Sale told George Burt, Canadian director of the UAW, that Ford would expand in Windsor to the tune of $32,500,000 with more jobs than before. It was the same amount of money going to Oakville and would, as the company's in-house newspaper, *Ford Graphic* explained, "provide the largest and most up-to-date automotive engine plant in Canada; the most advanced foundry and a machine shop that will rank second-to-none."

In January, 1953, Ford explained the expansion through full-page ads in 80 daily newspapers across the country. They featured aerial views of the Windsor and Oakville plants. Sale also broadcast a special New Year's message on the "Ford Theatre" program in English and French. It was heard by 2,500,000 Canadians.

the last hold-outs, was finally certified as workers voted 7,000-4,500 in favour. There were celebrations but also tears from older employees who equated allegiance to the UAW as disloyalty to the company.

However there was dissatisfaction with the first contract. Many workers felt pressured into accepting company terms because of the war and the need to maintain production. At war's end the union decided it was time for tough bargaining. Talks collapsed and on September 21, 1945, Ford entered into the most disastrous strike in its history. The Windsor Police Deparment was strengthened with arrival of RCMP and OPP officers. Fights flared at the plant gates as police clashed with pickets during the 99-day ordeal. The principal issue was security, which the union eventually won.

In 1949, Rhys M. Sale became president, holding the post

Ford observed its 50th anniversary in 1953 and, to celebrate, the company sponsored free "Music Under the Stars" concerts in Jackson Park. On Aug 22, 1954, its 50th anniversary, Ford presented a "Golden Jubilee Panorama", a two-hour Ford Story full of drama, music and pageantry with 200 actors on the largest stage in Windsor.

Twenty-one scholarships of $500 each over three years were offered to children of Ford workers who couldn't afford to go to university.

Ford remained in Windsor as a parts manufacturer, building transmissions and rear axles. Then, in November, 1968, the company spent $100,000,000 to convert Plant Two to produce engines. Another engine plant costing $500,000,000 was built in 1970 and, by the end of the decade, Ford was Canada's second-largest car company, with sales totalling $9.6 billion.

Weathering the '80s was tough on the auto industry. At Ford, the advertising slogan became "Quality is Job One." Quality improved 65 percent, emission controls were reduced by 90 percent and the cars featured air bags and other safety devices.

In 1992, James G. O'Connor, a New York native, became chief executive officer, the first American-born corporate head since Edsel Ford. The same year, the company lost $364,000,000, the worst deficit in its 88-year history.

By 1993, Ford announced a $1.3-billion expansion for Windsor. One billion was earmarked for Engine Plant Two, renamed the Windsor Engine Plant, where three new truck engines would be built.

One hundred million dollars was set aside to expand and equip the Essex Aluminum Plant, which was originally built in 1981 next to the Essex Engine Plant. The aluminum plant would produce cast-aluminum cylinder heads for the new truck engines.

This Ford Coupelet (circa 1915) was offered for sale at $730, FOB, "Ford, Ontario". The top was lowered for sunny-day driving, or raised against inclement weather.

Another $200 million would go toward the building of a new aluminum casting plant which would turn out aluminum cylinder blocks for a new generation of engines. This west-side facility is expected to employ about 350 people by 1995 and is three times larger than originally planned. A new research and development centre nearby would operate as a pilot plant for Ford's casting division.

The plan was to turn out 1,000,000 castings annually, which would contribute to improved fuel efficiency with lighter engines. It was a first for Ford's world-wide operation and a vote of confidence for the future of the auto industry in Windsor.

"Model T" — The "Tin Lizzie" Created A Nation Of Motorists

It had some of the characteristics of a mule, the patience of a camel, the courage of a bull terrier, and a whimsical hostility to the human race.

They wrote songs and poems, cracked jokes, laughed or lamented when they saw it coming. It looked like a top-hat on wheels. It was the car everyone loved to hate.

It was Henry Ford's "Model T" — more affectionately known as the "Tin Lizzie", even though there was less than half a pound of tin in the whole thing. Its presence introduced the word "Flivver" to our language, derived from the joke that riding in one "was good f'r the liver."

Like it or leave it, the "T" was legendary. It created a nation of motorists.

Ford designed his Model "T" during the winter of 1906 in his workshop on the third floor of the Piquette Plant in Michigan. The workshop was a tiny room, barely large enough for the car, a few power tools, blackboard and rocking chair. He devoted 15 hours a day to the project before testing it on Detroit streets. It wasn't just transportation, it was the first car to create brand loyalty, and Ford was pleased.

It was also a target for cynics and critics. Aldous Huxley irreverently referred to the Model T in his book, *Brave New World*. The Ford was a symbol of fulfillment and the meaning of life, the perfect creation. Huxley's people crossed themselves with the sign of the "T" in the year of Our Ford. "Ford's in his Flivver, all's right with the world."

There was even a joke book called "Fun-about Fords."

Ford Runabout

Overshadowed by the sheer size and power of today's 18-wheelers, truck transportation has come a long way since this Model "T" hit the dusty roads in 1922.

Q. "Why is it called a runabout?"
A. "Because it runs about a mile without stopping."

• • •

A farmer tears the tin roof off his barn and mails it to Ford. The company replies:

"Your Model T is the worst wreck we've ever seen. It will take us two weeks to fix it."

• • •

In time the jokes had more bite.
"What does the Model T use for shock absorbers?"
"The passengers..."

• • •

Ford, who understood marketing and promotion, also had fun with the car. He advertised it by driving up mountains or the steps of the YMCA. He sponsored the "Model T Rodeo",

1919: Ford's Model T — also known as the "Tin Lizzie" — was truly a mechanical workhorse... a power plant to serve many needs. Here, workmen hoisted the back end, attached a drive belt to the rear wheel and — presto! — enough power to drive a circular wood saw.

using a car instead of a horse, and even balanced it on a huge teeter-totter to demonstrate its control.

The Model T was Henry Ford's dream car — a car for the multitude. The booklet that came with it in 1914 summed it up, apparently in Ford's words:

"I will build a motor car for the multitudes. It shall be large enough for the family, but small enough for the unskilled individual to easily operate — and it shall be light in weight that it may be economical in maintenance. It will be built of honest materials — by the best workmen that money can hire — after the simplest designs that modern engineering can devise. But it shall be so low in price that the man of moderate means may own one — and enjoy with his family, the blessings of happy hours spent in God's great open spaces."

The Model T lived up to the dream.

Most cars were expensive toys for the rich, but the Tin Lizzie was affordable, durable and versatile.

Farmers loved the car because it was a workhorse. With the rear wheel jacked up and spinning, it could be rigged with a power takeoff to saw wood, pump water, mill feed or generate electricity. The four-seater was large enough to hold a farmer's milk cans. It was light with wide wheels which didn't bog down in mud. On Sunday it could be dusted off to take the family to church. By 1917 farmers bought 60 per cent of all cars in Canada — most were the Model T.

At first, the cost of the Flivver was relatively high — $1,150 — but once production methods improved, prices dropped. By 1912, the price was slashed to $750 and it hit an all-time low in

1925: A solitary Ford worker shapes a body component for a Model T.

the whole transmission, which meant the person starting the car ran the risk of being run over or suffering a sprained wrist, broken arm or strained back!

On cold mornings people chanted a Lewis Carroll parody:

Speak harshly to your little Ford,
And kick it when it freezes,
It does it only to annoy,
Because it knows it teases.

In World War One, Canadian troops used the Model T as an ambulance in France. They nicknamed it the Galloping Bedstead, but Colonel T. E. Lawrence — Lawrence of Arabia — praised the Lizzie as one of the few cars suited to desert warfare.

Ford's car had a simple chassis, wheels, tires and oil lamps. Buyers got a mechanical skeleton — if they wanted a windshield, lights, speedometer, starter, temperature gauge and bumpers — they paid extra.

The "T" came in five body styles. Early models were red or gray but in June, 1909, they were painted Brewster Green with black trim and red striping — until Ford's no-nonsense black took over.

The Canadian "T" differed slightly from its American cousin. It had its own, made-in-Canada flavour. In the United States, because of the brake lever position, there was no door on the driver's side of the open car — it was just a dummy outline. In

1925 of $395 for a roadster — without a starter — which cost another $85.

It was honest marketing with the savings passed on to consumers. The philosophy also benefitted shareholders. Four hundred and fifty-eight cars were produced in the first year and, the following year, stockholders received huge dividends as share prices rose dramatically.

Devoted owners swore their Model Ts quivered, snuffled and nudged them as if they were alive. Early models came equipped with a hand crank to start the car. Sometimes, if the brake didn't catch, the car edged forward, forcing the person cranking to brace it with a shoulder.

For cold starting it was best to jack up the rear wheel — otherwise it gummed up the clutch plates. It helped to crank

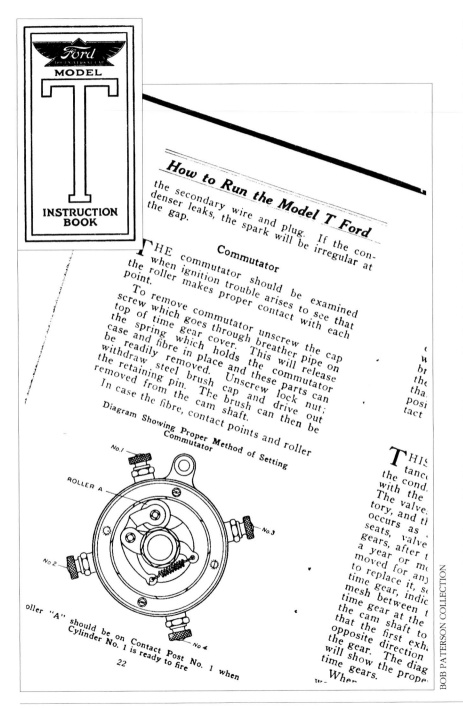

Canada, both doors opened, allowing either right or left-hand steering, depending on provincial requirements.

This Ford was a quirky little car. It didn't have a water pump because Ford figured that warm water rises by itself. Owners swore it could boil like a samovar.

The first electric lights worked off a low-tension magneto hooked into the engine flywheel. The lights brightened when the car went fast. Climbing a steep hill reduced the beam to an orange glow. Travelling downhill meant a floodlit stretch of road.

The tone of the horn also varied with the engine speed. Blow the horn at the wrong moment, the driver risked stalling. As if that wasn't enough to challenge the patience of a driver, Ford's Flivver had a gravity-feed fuel system. Drivers often had to negotiate hills in reverse to fuel the engine.

Introduced in 1908, the little car wheezed along for 18 years. Roughly 758,000 Canadians bought new Lizzies and thousands more were purchased second-hand. The brass radiator models prior to 1916 are prized by collectors.

During the Model T era, the Windsor plant became the biggest auto factory in the British Empire. By 1913, Ford was making 27 cars a day. Some people said that Ford would flood the market, yet he couldn't keep up with demand.

While the "T" was synonymous with Ford, there was a pretender — a "Model T" truck, built in 1918, by Chevrolet. It didn't come close to the popularity of the Ford car and only 27 were made and sold in Canada.

The Tin Lizzie may have been the best car for the money ever built, but its popularity couldn't last and Ford himself may have been responsible for its demise. Ford could be uncompromising and obstinate, refusing to accept changes, except for minor components.

For example, difficulties starting the car because of a low-tension timer could have been solved. The two-speed transmission was outdated by 1912. The car's two-wheel, low-power brakes and non-styling had no place amid the relative sophistication of the Roaring 20s.

By 1924, buyers wanted bright colours to match their flamboyant lifestyles. They rebelled against Henry's "any-colour-so-long-as-it's-black" philosophy.

For a time Ford refused to make changes, fearing they would undermine his concept of mass production. Change meant retooling at higher cost and lower profit. In the end he conceded, introducing wire wheels, electric starters and battery-electric lighting instead of the low-powered magneto.

The changes were too few, too late. The Model T led the market for 13 years, but Chevrolet took over and Ford withdrew the car. Even though parts could be bought in any country store, the Tin Lizzie's day was done. It was replaced by the new Model A.

Ford never fully understood what happened. Years later he said, "the only thing wrong with that car was that people stopped buying it." In a last-ditch appeal in the U.S., ads for the 1924 Model T were designed to appeal to women, proclaiming that it was as easy to operate as the kitchen range.

The "T" remained popular in Canada for two more years, in fact, the greatest sales volume was in 1926, the last full year of production.

That was the year Windsor police bought a Model T touring car which they ran for eight years. Police assigned to the vehicle had to work an extra hour because it was considered an "easy" job. It was also cold in winter because the car didn't have a heater or side window glass.

Ford Motor Company made almost 15,500,000 Model T's worldwide — a global sales record that held until the 1970s when it was eclipsed by the Volkswagen Beetle.

"Young Henry" Made Things Happen

Luck and timing had much to do with the success of many car companies, but there were other, more important elements necessary for survival — sheer drive and determination, bordering on desperation, by those involved.

Henry Ford put it all together. "Young Henry", considered "one of the boys", was always ready with a joke and was full of impish tricks. He was also an obsessive worker, a master mechanic, a driving force, never slow to slip out of his jacket to work with his men. He expected

The young man who was destined to put the world on wheels, Henry Ford was 33 years old when this photograph of his first car, the famed "quadricycle" was taken in 1896. The car, powered by a two-cylinder, four-cycle engine, had an electric bell up front to warn pedestrians — the fashion of trolleys of the day.

FORD OF CANADA ARCHIVES

FORD OF CANADA ARCHIVES

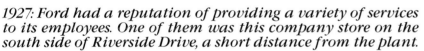

1927: Ford had a reputation of providing a variety of services to its employees. One of them was this company store on the south side of Riverside Drive, a short distance from the plant.

The Universal Car Agency, founded in 1912, was the first Ford dealership in Windsor. It was owned by John Duck and Donald McGregor, brother of Gordon McGregor.

the same commitment of others.

Ford knew that things didn't "just happen" — he made them happen. When necessary, he even did his own test-driving on the ice of Lake St. Clair to show that his cars could take it, while achieving speed records. Two tests included his famous "999" and "Arrow".

Although not comfortable as a test driver, Ford realized that speed tests created interest, financial support and increased sales. One day his driver, Barney Oldfield, didn't show for a run, so Ford took the car on the one-mile straight-away himself. He called it "the most frightening experience" of his life.

"The ice was seamed with fissures which I knew were going to mean trouble the minute I got speed up... With every fissure the car leaped into the air. I never knew how it was coming down. When I wasn't up in the air, I was skidding, but

somehow I stayed topside-up and on the course, making a record that went all over the world."

He was shaken when he finally stopped, but he had done the mile in 36 seconds!

• • •

Building a string of reliable dealerships was essential to the health of the company, and running a dealership was not taken lightly. "Head-office" warnings were issued on proper conduct, including this timely gem:

"Don't get yourself up like some young sport whose chief aim in life is to smoke up a half dozen packs and take his lady friends riding. Selling cars is a dignified profession; dress and act the part."

• • •

Amherstburg history buff and author David Botsford described his first trip in 1908 in a five-passenger car driven by

McGregor. The Ford had a bulb-horn, brass headlights, a fold-down top and no doors on the front.

They left the Botsford farm, travelled through Amherstburg, heading along the riverfront. When the car encountered a horse, McGregor stopped to allow the frightened animal to pass. Later, when he met a woman driving a buggy, he stopped and graciously led the woman's horse past.

As darkness approached, McGregor turned on the valves of the Presto-Lite tanks, struck a match and the road was bathed in light. Botsford returned home "thrilled to the bone with the experience."

• • •

In 1913, for the first time, women worked in the Canadian operations. On May 5, Mildred Wood became the first of 230 women hired by G. W. Hillman, the foreman of the magneto department.

The line had just been converted to the new principle of mass production. Flywheels were assembled on a moving line and for 10 years, women wound, soldered and taped magneto coils. The job was eliminated in 1924 and the women were transferred to the upholstery department. That lasted only a short time before they were banished from the plant.

On his retirement after 44 years, Hillman maintained that women created extra problems because he had to provide special chairs, lunch room and washrooms as well as extend their lunch period from a half hour to a full hour. When a woman arrived in her party dress and refused to change into her working smock, she was fired the next day.

• • •

During World War One, the company offered help to Ford owners at home by introducing service cars in major cities. Twenty vehicles assisted with problems ranging from lost keys to empty fuel tanks.

The service cars were equipped with searchlights, fire extinguishers, tire pumps, and even a spare steering wheel. An anti-freezing device, attached to the exhaust, thawed cars on winter mornings. The service men wore Ford uniforms.

FORD OF CANADA ARCHIVES

Blood
Brother
to an unknown patriot

He steps away from his daily work, rolls up his sleeve and cheerfully donates his blood — so that some unknown brother or sister may come back again from under the black shadow of death. Through the efficient services of the Canadian Red Cross, his blood is speedily transported in dried form to be used for transfusions in Britain, Russia, Egypt or wherever war's shock takes its toll.

Ford of Canada honours all blood donors; especially those who come from the ranks of Canada's great army of production workers. At Windsor, in the Ford of Canada blood clinic, many thousands of Ford workers have already made more than 7000 blood donations.

So that this great work — binding Canada to her brothers and sisters of other nations with the strongest of all ties — may carry on, the Canadian Red Cross needs your help.

The need for Red Cross help is now greater than ever. Let Canada's response be quick and generous.

$10,000,000 NEEDED NOW GIVE— HUMAN SUFFERING IS GREATER THAN EVER

This Advertisement contributed by

FORD MOTOR COMPANY OF CANADA, LIMITED

Ford-sponsored blood-donor clinics generated thousands of units during the war years.

FORD OF CANADA ARCHIVES

• • •

In 1916, Ford Motor went to the aid of the newly formed 241st Battalion, Scottish Borderers. The Canadian government refused to buy kilts for the battalion, so Ford picked up the bill. The MacGregor tartan was selected in honour of Walter McGregor Q.C., commanding officer, and his uncle Gordon, founder of Ford of Canada. The tartan is red with green and a white stripe.

• • •

That same year, the company opened a school to teach English to employees. Classes were held after work, free of charge. They could also study math, if they paid 10 cents for the text book.

• • •

Ford workers gained a reputation for charity during World War One when they contributed $76,000 to the Red Cross and the Canadian Patriotic Fund — an average of $30 per employee. The generosity was repeated during World War Two when Ford workers bought Canada Victory Bonds worth $14,000,000.

• • •

The company put everything it had into the war effort. The Ford sign, said to be the largest of its kind, was dismantled and recycled for war use. Ford workers also salvaged steel street car rails. During the war, Ford maintained an extensive advertising campaign featuring workers and the company's military production. Some showed Allied forces on the offensive with pictures of battle manoeuvres so accurate they were used by military authorities for instructional purposes.

In 1946 Ford reprinted the ads in a hard cover book titled: *Ford of Canada in Wartime.* It was presented to Ford employees returning from overseas, to show what the company had done to support the Allied forces. It was accompanied by a congratulatory letter.

Ford advertising wasn't limited to the macho battle cries of war — there was also a poetic side to Ford ads:

The Ford V-8s, a Windsor basketball team sponsored by Ford, won the Canadian Basketball Championship, then represented Canada in the 1936 Berlin Olympics. They won the Silver Medal, losing the final game to the Americans 19-8.
Members of the V-8s shown in this photo are: Gord Aitchison, with the ball; Harry Heydon, Malcolm Wiseman, Jimmy Stewart, Irving Meretsky, Tom Pendlebury, Norm Dawson, Don Gray, Stanley Nantais, Ernie Williams and coach Gordon Fuller.

The honk of the horn has a magical note
That charms all your troubles away;
And the hum of the motor invites you to go
Where the blossoms and birds are at play.
There is somewhere a classy new Model T Ford
Awaiting my hand on the wheel,
So put on your hat and together we'll go
And purchase this automobile.

• • •

A street car that took many employees to and from work was called the "Ford Special" or "Galloping Gus". At first, it ran to the Crown Inn, opposite the Walkerville Railway Station, but by 1913, it carried the workers right to the plant gates. On cold winter mornings, the men often had to push Galloping Gus over the Peabody Bridge. The Ford Special, or Trolley 101, came to an inglorious end in 1922 when it was demolished by a shunting freight train.

• • •

Ford opened a trade school in 1936, a four-year course for employees under 21. Only one in three applicants was accepted. Subjects taught by senior Ford employees included tool-and-die, industrial electricity, metal fabrication and drafting. Hundreds graduated and 75 per cent stayed with Ford. In 1948, the course was recognized by the American Society of Tool Engineers, the first such honour for a Canadian firm.

The world knows that the Ford Motor Company built cars and trucks — but less well known is that, for a time, the company produced passenger buses as well. The Sandwich, Windsor & Amherstburg Railway Company began purchasing them in the late 1930s and, by the end of World War Two, had a fleet of 177. Six of the 27-passenger vehicles are visible in this vibrant street scene, looking north on Ouellette Avenue from Wyandotte Street. This rare photograph was taken by Sid Lloyd, one of Windsor's very early press photographers.

In blustery winter weather, before making their passenger runs, the bus drivers cleared their routes with these Ford trucks.

Ford Trucks and Buses Found Favour With Windsor's Transit Company

In 1926, the first Windsor-built buses were used on city streets.

The four vehicles were a familiar sight on Lincoln Road, Howard Avenue and Wyandotte. They were built and owned by Gotfredson Truck Company of Windsor and leased to the Sandwich, Windsor and Amherstburg Railway (SW&A), which provided the service. The fare was 10 cents; the venture wasn't profitable and the leasing agreement was cancelled in 1931.

When W. H. Furlong became chairman of SW&A in 1938, he opted for an all-bus system and chose the Ford transit bus as the standard vehicle. The first three buses replaced the trolleys serving Amherstburg and the trolleys also disappeared from Windsor streets as each Ford bus was delivered. The fare was still only 10 cents.

One tradition kept alive by the SW&A was the funeral coach. It was Number 76, with "Funeral" displayed on the destination sign. Windows were draped in black and it was used to take bereaved families and friends to the cemetery.

The SW&A was also known for its fleet of snowplows and sand spreaders, which until 1958 kept routes clear during the winter.

Buses were used extensively during World War Two, when there were restrictions on gasoline, tires and private cars. Ridership peaked in 1945 when factories worked 24 hours a day. By war's end, there were 177, 27-passenger Fords in the fleet — the largest Ford fleet in Canada.

With a return to peacetime, SW&A retired the Fords and bought bigger units. Ford-built buses were off Windsor streets by 1954.

The Years Of Discovery

Plant Number 2, built in 1922, was mothballed in 1990. It was then gutted and retooled to produce fuel-efficient truck engines.

Here Today, Gone Tomorrow — Phoenix Rises From The Ashes

The automotive industry has always been the most fickle, volatile, unpredictable and mercurial of any major manufacturing industry. It is driven by the need to produce new models. Companies are slaves to advancing techology. Change is their nature.

Given the astronomical size of the industry, and cyclical nature of the business, changes come frequently and often with dramatic impact. Either a plant opens, with hundreds of new jobs and millions of dollars committed, or a plant closes and hundreds are suddenly out of work.

Ford's plans to close its Engine Plant Number Two, on Cadillac Street created a sense of dismay, though not total surprise. After all, the dowdy, 70-year-old brick building — large enough to house 14 football fields — was down-at-the-heels. Four generations of workers toiled under the green-tinted skylights, which cast an eerie glow into the night sky.

First opened in 1922 for parts production, Plant Two, has played many roles over the years. During World War Two it produced 400,000 bomber wings, landing gears, parts for Universal Carriers and Bren guns. Peacetime production turned to transmissions, wheels, brakes, and, in 1970, engines — eventually turning out half a million a year.

The plant was a city within a city boasting the biggest tool shop in the British Commonwealth, employing 1,000 people.

In the mid-to-late 1930s, Ford's Plant Two was used as a feeder plant, where partial body assembly was carried out before the cars were moved to Plant One for final assembly.

FORD OF CANADA ARCHIVES

It's said that on pay days, a nearby bank became, temporarily, one of the richest in Canada.

As with every segment of the industry, Plant Two had its upheavals. In the '30s there was no guarantee that work in the morning meant work in the afternoon. Smoking and talking on the production line were prohibited, and supervisors, whose bonuses relied on production, played one shift against another.

When jobs were scarce, offering to shovel snow or cut grass for someone higher up, or a discreet gift of the local brew ensured work at the plant.

The economic climate in 1980 was hard on the auto industry and Plant Two was closed for a year as the company rationalized its operations. An unexpected strengthening in the North American truck market prompted Ford to reopen the plant temporarily. It was only supposed to last a year to produce components for the Cleveland engine plant, but it kept going until 1990, when Ford announced its closure again.

Plant Two was a cornerstone in the northwest part of old Ford City — sometimes referred to as the Factory District. In this new, high-tech age, there seemed little chance of breathing life into it again.

Six hundred and seventy people — one sixth of all Ford workers in Windsor — were jobless. Many had up to 13 years' seniority. Some were hired as summer replacements elsewhere. For most, the future was bleak.

In the end, 125 skilled tradesmen were left to gut the old place, spending more than a year salvaging heavy machinery, presses and broachers used to shave metal.

Suddenly, Ford reversed its decision, saying that, instead of mothballing the plant, $1 billion would be spent refurbishing it to produce a new generation of light, fuel-efficient, truck engines.

Work started immediately, and like a fairytale Phoenix rising from the ashes, the plant was stripped down to its steel girders and refurbished with a new roof and walls.

A new second floor would house offices, cafeteria and showers. Fresh, modern wall cladding would enhance the plant's appearance and worker-friendly rubber mats would replace the old concrete floor.

Even employee attitudes are likely to change, as the traditional, structured system of supervision disappears in favour of a new team environment. Ford officials targeted October 1994 to have the first engine off the line. With luck, 1,000 workers could be on the job in 1995.

If all goes according to plan, the plant's reincarnation could take it through another quarter-century — providing work for another generation of Ford workers in this, the most fickle of all industries.

This panoramic view, taken during the early 1950s, shows Chrysler's first plant and office in Canada — the former Maxwell-Chalmers Motor Company of Canada. It was located on Tecumseh Road East, between McDougall and Mercer streets.

Walter Percival Chrysler Bet Everything On His Youthful Dream

It takes genius, guts and perseverance to survive in the car business. It takes someone willing to back his own hunches, ride long shots, and bet on dreams with little fear of the odds.

Walter Percival Chrysler was that kind of guy.

Chrysler's great great grandfather was the first settler in what is now Chatham, Ontario. His father travelled from Chatham to Kansas in a covered wagon. A Canadian-once-removed, Chrysler was born in Kansas in 1875. He became a sweeper with the Union Pacific Railway but had such a love of machinery that he built his own tools by hand when he was only 17.

In 1905, the impressionable young railroad mechanic blew $5,000 — a full year's pay — on his first car, a white Locomobile with red upholstery and brass metal-work. He only had $700 to his name and it would take three years to pay the debt, but he had to have the car. This broad-shouldered midwesterner saw automobiles as the transportation of the future.

Chrysler spent hours taking his car apart to learn what made it tick. He showed similar zeal in 1911, when he took the biggest gamble of his life, leaving his job as works manager for a locomotive company in Pittsburgh, to join the Buick Motor Company in Flint, Michigan.

His salary fell from $12,000 to $6,000, but it was his destiny. Building cars is what Chrysler wanted to do.

For the next two years, Chrysler worked around the clock making improvements. He replaced heat-treated axles with cold rolled ones; used wood reinforced with steel, instead of all-wood bodies. Within five years, Chrysler was president and general manager of Buick, and first vice-president of GM in charge of production.

Under Chrysler's supervision, Buick's daily production rose from 40 cars to more than 600. By the time he left, profits had risen to $46,000,000.

By 1919, Chrysler was one of the highest paid managers in

the business but, when he wasn't allowed to run the Buick division the way he wanted, he retired, a wealthy man at 45.

By then, cars were to Chrysler what cards are to gamblers. In 1920, a group of bankers talked Chrysler into reorganizing the over-extended, Willys Overland Corporation, offering an astounding $1,000,000 a year for two years. He couldn't resist and became executive vice-president of Willys which he saved from bankruptcy.

Chrysler's stock as a trouble-shooter skyrocketed and, in 1921, he became a $100,000 parttime consultant to Maxwell Motors, an American firm with a subsidiary plant in Windsor. Maxwell was highly successful, amalgamating dozens of smaller companies, but the competition was fighting back.

The Maxwell was advertised as the:

"New Good Maxwell, Perfectly Simple, Simply Perfect".

It boasted an electric starter, lights, a speedometer, gas gauge and tires good for 8,000 miles. It also had a reputation as a clinker.

In 1920, Percy Gomery, president of the Vancouver Auto Club took the car on a Montreal-Vancouver jaunt. It was supposed to be a leisurely trip across the northern United States. It didn't turn out that way.

The Maxwell bogged down in mud, collided with another car in the Rockies and Gomery was ticketed for speeding in Fort Garry (Winnipeg), Manitoba. When Gomery limped home, he hated the Maxwell and said so.

By 1921, the company sold only 16,000 cars in North America, compared to Ford's 900,000. It was $20 million in debt.

Chrysler began reversing Maxwell's fortunes by merging with Chalmers Motor Car Company, another American firm in financial difficulty. It, too, had a plant in Windsor. The new firm, called Maxwell-Chalmers, then Maxwell-Chrysler, was the forerunner of Chrysler Corporation.

Maxwell-Chalmers' roots in Windsor go back to 1916 when Maxwell Motors built a large passenger car and truck plant on Tecumseh Road between McDougall and Mercer. The city was already Canada's largest and most important auto manu-

Walter P. Chrysler, hired as a consultant by Maxwell Motors in 1921, merged that firm with Chalmers Motor Car Company. The new company was called Maxwell-Chalmers, then Maxwell-Chrysler, forerunner of Chrysler Corporation.

facturing centre! That same year, the Chalmers Motor Car Company of Canada began production on St. Luke Road in Ford City.

A headline in *The Evening Record* on February 8, 1916 reflects the optimism of the day.

Auto centre is going up here. Maxwell and Chalmers added to important group of industries.

By 1919, Maxwell was exporting 500 cars and 155 trucks per month to the British Isles, Ceylon, Egypt and the Indies, but its prosperity wouldn't last. Chrysler consolidated the two operations in the Maxwell plant. The Chalmers car was soon phased out and the Maxwell followed in July 1925. The last model was driven off the production line bedecked in flowers.

To revive the company, Chrysler picked a team of U.S.

designers to develop an entirely new car bearing the Chrysler name. They came up with a high-powered, six-cylinder car offered in nine body styles as the "Chrysler Six."

It was a sensation at the National Auto Show in New York. Priced at $750, it came with features previously found only on more expensive models.

Nineteen years after Chrysler gambled on his first car, he was in the driver's seat.

He reorganized the sales of Maxwell-Chalmers and negotiated a $50,000,000 loan allowing him to control the firm and put his car on the road.

John D. Mansfield, president of Maxwell-Chalmers, was named first vice-president of the Chrysler Corporation of Canada Limited, when the firm was founded in June, 1925 — 11 days after Chrysler in the U.S.

Before Iacocca, it cost Chrysler millions to stockpile thousands of unsold cars in open fields waiting to fill customer orders.

In Chrysler Canada's first year, 4,000 cars were built in Windsor by 181 employees. Within a year, production almost doubled with 243 employees. Two models were assembled here — a four and a six cylinder with starting prices of $1,240. The next year prices dropped to $930 and Chrysler became a major player.

In 1927, Chrysler leased the former Fisher Body plant on Edna Street in Walkerville. Chrysler was then able to assemble, paint and trim its own bodies at the Fisher site, freeing floor space in the Tecumseh Road plant for chassis assembly.

Chrysler also showcased his first luxury vehicle, the Imperial E-80. The car was clocked at 80 miles an hour and was the original North American "muscle" car, a trend-setter which took second place at the Belgian Grand Prix, a 24-hour grind for the finest cars in the world.

In 1928 Chrysler acquired Toronto's prestigious Dodge Brothers Company, as well as Graham Brothers of Canada, a truck manufacturer. Chrysler produced Dodge, DeSoto and Plymouth models and was poised for the Big Leagues. The company ranked third as an auto manufacturer.

Chrysler bought 70 acres on the south side of Tecumseh Road. The cornfield became the site of a huge passenger car assembly plant, the forerunner to Plant Number 3. It eventually became the nucleus of the Windsor assembly plant and company headquarters on Chrysler Centre.

Despite constant upgrading, the site at Tecumseh Road and McDougall was inadequate. Within four years production had soared to more than 25,000 vehicles while the work force topped 1,500.

The DeSoto Motor Corporation of Canada, a unit of Chrysler,

Chrysler Canada Presidents from Mansfield to Landry

JOHN D. MANSFIELD, President of Maxwell-Chalmers, was named First Vice-President of Chrysler Canada Limited when the firm was founded in June, 1925. Mansfield, a graduate of the School of Hard Knocks was raised on his father's cattle ranch in Missouri before gaining experience as a salesman in a Chicago stockyard and with the Durant-Dort Carriage Company of Michigan. When Walter Chrysler died in 1940, Mansfield succeeded him. Mansfield retired in 1942, became Chairman of the Board, and died of a heart attack within the year.

Mansfield

E. C. ROW, who served five years as Vice-President and General Manager of Chrysler Corporation of Canada was elected President on February 16, 1951. Row worked for Chrysler and Dodge in the U.S. and Canada for 34 years. He came to Canada in 1942, as Assistant to the President. In 1946, he was elected Vice-President and General Manager, the position he held until becoming President. Row was a driving force behind Chrysler's post-war expansion. Windsor's only expressway, on the city's south side, was named in his honour. He died in 1973.

Row

C. W. CHURCHILL was born in Detroit and began his career in the automotive industry in 1921 when he became Director of Sales of the Buick Division of General Motors. He came to Canada in 1934 as Vice-President of Chrysler Corporation of Canada Limited. He succeeded John Mansfield as President on January 5, 1942. He received the Order of the British Empire for Chrysler's production of artillery weapons at Sorel, Quebec. He was President of Chrysler Canada until, after suffering a heart attack in his office, he died on February 10, 1951 at 70.

Churchill

RON W. TODGHAM was born in Toronto, moved to Windsor in 1915. While studying at Walkerville Collegiate, he took summer jobs in the company mailing room and acted as chauffeur for Mansfield. After graduating from the University of Michigan he joined Chrysler Canada. He left in 1938 to run a dealership in Chatham but returned in 1955. He was elected Executive Vice-President in May 1956, and became the first Canadian-born President in July. He retired in September, 1975. He entered hospital for heart surgery, but died the day after Christmas at 65.

Todgham

C. O. (Syd) HURLY joined Chrysler Canada Ltd., as a clerk in the Toronto regional sales office in 1936. He held positions of increasing responsibility and in 1956 was appointed Vice-President — Sales and then Vice-President — Marketing in 1970; in 1974 he became an Executive Vice-President and on October 1, 1975 succeeded Todgham as President of Chrysler Canada. The following year he was named a Vice-President of Chrysler Corporation. He retired in 1979 and lives in Toronto.

Hurly

M. J. (MOE) CLOSS, colourful and charismatic, has been likened by some, as the Lee Iacocca of Canada. Born in Toronto, he started working for General Motors in 1945. He joined Chrysler in 1959. In 1979 he became Staff Executive for U.S. Automotive Sales and Marketing. In 1980 he returned to Canada as Executive Vice-President and became President and CEO of Chrysler Canada in July 1980. During his presidency he fought to take the company from the brink of financial disaster. He retired on December 31, 1989 and lives on the outskirts of Windsor.

Closs

DONALD H. LANDER. Born in Oshawa, Lander held a variety of sales positions with General Motors of Canada before joining Chrysler Canada in 1959 as Passenger Car Sales Manager. He spent the next 20 years climbing the corporate ladder and was elected President and CEO of Chrysler Canada on April 19, 1979. He retired the following year, joining DeLorean Motor Cars Limited in Belfast. He left DeLorean to become chairman of the board of directors and CEO of Canada Post.

Lander

G.Y. (YVES) LANDRY was born in Thetford Mines, Quebec and joined Chrysler Canada in Montreal in 1969. In 1977 he was appointed Manager — Merchandising at Chrysler Canada's head office in Windsor. In 1980 he was elected a Vice-President of Chrysler Canada Ltd and in 1988, was appointed General-Manager — International Sales and Marketing, Chrysler Motors. He played a key role in Chrysler's re-entry into world vehicle markets. He returned to Chrysler Canada as Executive Vice-President in 1989 and became president and CEO on January 1, 1990.

Landry

Driving early model cars might have been fun, but maintaining them was something of a chore. This snappy 1925-26 Chrysler Six had a complex system of daily and weekly lubricating duties to keep it running smoothly.

operated at Edna Street in 1929 and '30. It was probably just an office, as the DeSoto cars were built in the new Plant 3.

The first Dodge truck rolled off the line at the Tecumseh Road plant in 1931 and, four years later, was joined by the Fargo.

The year 1933 saw the introduction of the model series that Chrysler built specifically for the Canadian market. It was a small, low-priced Dodge, similar to a 1960 Plymouth Six.

Chrysler also developed his Airflow design. It was fashioned after fighter aircraft of the day, but looked like an overgrown Volkswagen. The car was known for its smooth ride and its uni-body design, the first of its kind. Its weight, styling and engineering were all adapted by other car makers after World War Two, but in the '30s it was ahead of its time. Only 29,000 models sold from 1934 to '37. Because of its

aerodynamic styling, some people feared it would take off if driven too fast.

Despite the Depression, Chrylser produced a record 30,000 cars and trucks in Canada in 1936, paving the way for construction of a $3,000,000 engine plant in Windsor.

The company also built one custom car in Canada, a seven-passenger convertible sedan for the 1939 Royal Visit. It was maroon, with dark blue upholstery and was based, appropriately, on the Chrysler Royal chassis.

Being an American company, Chrysler wasn't involved in military production during the early stages of World War Two, but when Americans entered the fray, Chrysler began producing its war arsenal — almost 181,000 supply and troop-carrying trucks as well as rocket tubes, shells, tracers, igniters and other gun parts.

At war's end, Chrysler got back to the car business and expanded its assembly plant. When it moved into a new administration building on Chrysler Centre in 1949, it marked a new era in auto manufacturing. Not only had production reached a record 64,000 cars and trucks, employment reached 5,600 workers. The company moved into second place behind GM with a 25 per cent market share.

During the next two decades Chrysler expanded, added new lines, changed its corporate name and image, and added thousands of square feet through construction or purchase.

In 1965, signing of the Auto Pact allowed Chrysler to make large shipments to the U.S. in exchange for foreign products. The company cut the number of models in half but increased production by 35 per cent.

By the late 1970s, Chrysler had entered a period of tough reckoning and reorganization.

Although Canadian sales were still up, the U.S. market shrivelled. The company, deeply in debt, entered the most critical period in its history. There was every likelihood it would simply die on the vine.

Recently fired by Ford, Lee Iacocca was parachuted in to salvage what was left. The company owed $160,000,000 while

Ford and GM were enjoying record sales. Iacocca discovered that his top executives were working in a vacuum; the company needed order and discipline. He said Chrysler quality "was so bad, dealers expected to rebuild the cars when they received them".

It became an international joke. Tonight Show host Johnny Carson said, "I don't know what's wrong at Chrysler, but it's the first time I ever heard anybody make a conference call to Dial-A-Prayer".

Iacocca fired 33 of his 35 U.S. vice-presidents and introduced just-in-time shipments of parts to reduce inventories.

Iacocca forced production to meet demands and millions of dollars worth of inventory was eliminated. A high-powered advertising campaign introduced rebates and gimmicks to get people into the showrooms. The 1979 annual report was printed in cost-saving black and white, and the company sold its overseas operations.

He then sold the tank plant in Detroit, laid off thousands of people and slashed costs everywhere.

In August, 1980, the Windsor engine plant shut down after putting out more than 8,000,000 units in 42 years. A year later, production began on a smaller New Yorker called the Chrysler Imperial, an expensive luxury car, offering a totally electronic instrument panel with computer activated digital readouts. It was built exclusively in Windsor.

Chrysler transferred its LeBarons, Diplomats and Caravelles to Windsor from St. Louis, Missouri. It was a mammoth undertaking. Thirty-six transports — 14 carrying oversized loads requiring special permits — arrived in sequence. Up to 1,500 employees were trained to handle 5,400 components to build the three styles. The move cost $8,000,000 and took one month from start to finish.

As company fortunes sagged, Iacocca set an example by dropping his salary to one-dollar-a-year, giving him leverage with the unions. He warned that he had jobs at $17 an hour but none at $20.

Iacocca's team asked suppliers to cut prices and allow more

The sagging fortunes of Chrysler Canada took a dramatic turn for the better when the company opened its new mini-van assembly plant (above) in 1983. Below, Lee Iacocca waves happily as he drives the first mini-van off the assembly line during the formal "roll-off" ceremony.

The first convertible — a 1963 Dodge — ever built by Chrysler Canada generated considerable interest when it came off the assembly line on September 18, 1962. The sign reads: "The first one — built by Canadians for Canadians."

time to pay. They asked governments in both countries for loan guarantees. They asked the unions for concessions.

Critics turned thumbs down, arguing that the marketplace should prevail. They forgot that it wasn't just Chrysler and its empoyees who would be devastated. Hundreds of others in dozens of plants would be sucked into the vortex.

Senior editors at *The Windsor Star*, aware of the life-and-death struggle, were preparing what they referred to as a "doomsday scenario" — a series of stories detailing the catastrophe to Windsor and supplier cities if Chrysler collapsed.

Morale at the company was low as a siege mentality developed. Chrysler even stopped cleaning sidewalks in front of the plant because there wasn't enough money.

Turbulence continued until 1982. Chrysler resurrected the convertible — the first since 1971. It caught on and rolled across the counry like a flash flood.

Also in 1982, work started on the largest and most expensive plant conversion in Chrysler Canada's history. It was a 220,000-square-foot addition to the south end of the Windsor assem-

Chrysler Milestones: 1955-1980

In 1955, Chrysler spent $29 million expanding the engine plant, powerhouse and engineering building. The company also produced its first V-8 engine in Canada and the following year, celebrated a milestone by producing more than 100,000 cars. Other milestones came quickly.

- 1956: Ron W. Todgham became the first Canadian-born president.
- 1959: Chrysler added the compact Plymouth Valiant.
- 1963: Shortened the corporate name to Chrysler Canada Limited and introduced the Pentastar logo.
- 1963: Added 200,000 square feet to the car plant. Introduced the gas turbine engine car.
- 1964: Bought Walker Metal Products Foundry and L. A. Young Spring and Wire in Windsor.

- 1966: Added 500,000 square feet to the car and truck plants.
- 1968: Opened a $3,000,000 waste treatment plant.
- 1973: Built a record of almost 300,000 vehicles.
- 1974: Broke ground for a light-truck assembly plant.
- 1976: Opened Pillette Road truck assembly plant, its sole source of full-size vans and wagons.
- 1977: Spent $40,000,000, adding 125,000 square feet to the engine plant and 68,000 feet to the Pillette Road plant.
- 1978: Closed the truck plant at McDougall and Tecumseh Road.
- 1980: The Imperial Quality Assurance Centre opened with Frank Sinatra, Gregory Peck and Lee Iacocca attending.

Chrysler Canada President M. J. (Moe) Closs stands proudly with his Chrysler workers as the one-millionth full sized van comes off the Pillette Road Truck Assembly Plant. The plant opened in January 1976. Beside Closs is Jerome B. York, then general manager of the Dodge Division of Chrysler Corporation.

bly plant to house a new paint shop.

Chrysler had a commitment to Canada. The company promised to invest $700 million and provide 16,000 jobs by 1984 in order to get a $200-million government loan guarantee. The money was used to cover half the cost of conversion of the mini-van wagon plant.

By 1983 Chrysler was back on its feet and Iacocca, like Walter Chrysler before him, took to hyping his own products, saying with all the charisma and confidence he could muster:

"If you can find a better car — buy it."

Stock prices rebounded from about $3 to $35.

In May, the company produced its 5,000,000th car at the Windsor assembly plant, a white New Yorker Fifth Avenue. On June 10, 1983, Chrysler Canada President M. J. (Moe) Closs drove the last Windsor-built, rear-wheel drive passenger car off the line marking the end of an era. The 2,500,000-square-foot factory underwent major renovations for automated production of the all-new T-115 Van-Wagon and Mini-Ram Vans.

Though the conversion cost Chrysler $400 million it emerged as the first domestic car maker to build van-wagons, stealing a march on the competition. Windsor became the sole source of front-wheel drive mini-vans in the 1980s.

Construction started June 10 and by June 20 the plant was

stripped to the walls. In July, state-of-the-art technlogy was installed including 125 robots. The first employees were recalled in September and on October 7, the first T-115 Magic Wagon rolled off the assembly line.

The Windsor Star helped celebrate the occasion by toasting Chrysler at a festive reception at Willistead Manor.

By 1984, a year before Chrysler's 60th birthday in Canada, the company was Windsor's largest employer and taxpayer — the only automaker still producing vehicles in Windsor. The company reported record profits and paid its loans. Daily production hit 1,500 cars with more than 12,000 employees building 400,000 vehicles a year.

One year later, the former Maxwell factory where Chrysler Canada was born was brought down.

In 1987, Chrysler bought American Motors, which became the Jeep/Eagle Division of the company. It included two car

Just-in-time production practices reduced the need to maintain large, expensive inventories of parts — but sometimes serious logistical problems developed. In 1991, the Ambassador Bridge was blockaded by angry truck drivers protesting government actions. When the flow of parts was suddenly shut down, Chrysler brought them in by helicopter to keep assembly lines moving.

Award-winning Windsor sculptor Chris Rees was commissioned to create this bust, an excellent likeness of Chrysler President Lee Iacocca.

assembly and three parts plants near Toronto.

To mark the full extent of the turn-around, Chrysler became the first auto company to win the Canada Award for Business Excellence for production of its mini-van. It was a government award for producing a quality product.

By this point, more than 4,000 employees produced over 1,000 mini-vans a day in two shifts.

In 1992, the Pillette Road Truck Plant in Windsor underwent a $100-million refurbishing for a new van program to start the following year. The plant was shut down three weeks in December to produce a new full-size van wagon.

As a further indication of a turn-around in the industry, in March 1993, Chrysler announced it would spend $600 million to upgrade the old engine plant to produce a new stretch version of the mini-van. The conversion meant a new body plant and paint shop with more welding robots. No new jobs were created, but it demonstrated Chrysler's commitment to Windsor.

The conversion would take two years, with production beginning in 1995.

Preparing to step down, Iacocca introduced the new LH supercars, the Chrysler Concorde, Intrepid and Eagle Vision, catering to a wide range of tastes from "sporty" to "conventional".

He wanted another winner:

"When it's your last turn at bat, it's sure nice to hit a home run."

The ancient carriage factory (above) at Enniskillen, Ontario, pictured in 1869, was the humble birthplace of the McLaughlin family enterprises that grew into what is now GM of Canada. From here they moved into a larger complex in Oshawa, which burned. Following the fire in 1899, the company moved into temporary quarters at Gananoque (below) where business was carried on until a new plant could be built.

Founder of General Motors, "Mr. Sam" — One Very Proud Canadian

In Canada, the names General Motors and R. S. (Sam) McLaughlin are inseparable.

Mr. Sam, or The Colonel, as he was affectionately called, owned the McLaughlin Motor Car Company Limited of Oshawa. He had a voice of brass, a body of iron, a heart of gold — and was one of Canada's most successful automotive pioneers.

The McLaughlin automotive history began in the 1860s when Mr. Sam's father founded McLaughlin Carriage Works. Young Sam was born to the carriage-making trade but, as time passed, he saw the potential of the automobile and the threat it posed to his future.

"Mr. Sam" McLaughlin received his L.L.D. from York University at age 95

Although Sam couldn't convince his father to move fully into the car business, he was allowed to study the potential. He packed his bags and headed for Detroit to meet leaders in the new industry. In 1907 Mr. Sam signed an agreement to build a car using a Buick engine. He called it "The McLaughlin" and built 154 that year.

The start-up was so successful that Mr. Sam switched entirely in 1908 when he took over the family firm, and was on his way to becoming Canada's biggest and most successful auto manufacturer. He renamed his automobile the McLaughlin-Buick, a household name and one of the best known Canadian-made cars.

Mr. Sam was responsible for several industry firsts, including the first hand-operated windshield wiper in 1909. Three

GM's huge Windsor Transmission Plant, which fronts on Kildare Road and straddles Walker Road, produces front wheel drive transmissions for cars and the Lumina Van.

years later he introduced the first automatic wiper. His cars were the first to have brake lights and an adjustable front seat.

By the end of World War One, Mr. Sam's dominance was challenged by the growing popularity of other car makers. The used-car market was also maturing. Buyers started with less expensive models and traded up. Dozens of young car companies were going under and Mr. Sam feared his would follow.

He decided to team up with GM because the company's philosophy matched his own — produce a car for every purse and purpose.

General Motors was incorporated in the U.S. in 1908 by American industrialist William Crapo Durant. It became a holding company with over 30 divisions including Buick, Oldsmobile, Cadillac, Oakland and Chevrolet as well as countless parts and supply companies including Fisher Body and Champion Spark Plug.

GM's Canadian interests started to evolve in 1915 when the Chevrolet Motor Car Company of Canada was established under the McLaughlin banner. Three years later, McLaughlin and Canadian Chevrolet merged into General Motors of Canada, with Mr. Sam as president and his brother George as vice-president.

Even after the merger, Mr. Sam exerted a strong influence on the company, fighting to maintain a Canadian identity and insisting that his cars be built by Canadians using Canadian metals and hardwoods.

His slogan: "It's better because it's Canadian" appeared with a maple leaf logo on all advertising in Canada.

Later advertising read: "Better cars are being built — McLaughlin is building them."

In the U.S., McLaughlin's car was known as the Dominion Built Car, or the Empire Product. Canadians strongly identified with the McLaughlin name and, when GM tried to phase it out, sales plunged. When the McLaughlin name resurfaced, sales picked up. It was a signal that McLaughlin meant more to Canadians than Buick, then a prestigious name in the U.S.

In 1937, two special McLaughlin-Buicks were built for the style-conscious Prince of Wales. The cars gained royal attention because of Mr. Sam's pride in workmanship and his boast that all his products had a Canadian flavour. For example, the Canadian Oakland featured a walnut dash and little maple leaves on the hub caps.

Despite Mr. Sam's efforts, GM Canada became more and more Americanized and the McLaughlin name finally disappeared from the car line-up by 1942.

Prior to 1930, the only Windsor connection involved parts production. Fisher Auto Body in Detroit was affiliated with GM and, in 1919, opened on St. Luke Road to produce car bodies. The Fisher Auto Body Corporation of Canada had been making Ford auto bodies, but its GM agreement allowed it to double its capacity.

In 1921, GM Canada established Canadian Products Limited, a subsidiary on Walker Road. It was the company's principal source of engines and axles, which were shipped to Oshawa for assembly. The Walker Road and St. Luke sites were both closed in 1923

The '20s were boom years for GM, Ford's chief rival. It also underwent a major expansion to accommodate the export market to Britain. Over one third of its 57,000 vehicles went overseas by 1925. At the peak, in 1928, GM produced 82,000 cars.

In 1930, for the first time, GM hired 575 men to assemble Chevrolet and Pontiac cars and trucks on Walker Road. Assembly lasted only one year before production reverted to Oshawa. With the Depression, production plunged and the Walker Road plant retooled for engine production.

GMC trucks and buses were assembled at the Fisher Body plant under the auspices of GM Truck and Coach of Canada. Canadian production returned to Oshawa in 1932, the worst year of the Depression for GM. The Walker Road plant continued producing engines and axles, concentrating on engines after 1935 when axle production also moved to Oshawa. It was a period of consolidation.

GM sponsored three Parades of Progress, a spinoff of the GM Science and Technology display first presented at the 1933 Chicago World's Fair. The parades started in Florida with a huge caravan of eight red and white vans. Canvas awnings linked six of them, forming walk-through exhibits featuring a ping-pong game in stereophonic sound, a microwave oven that fried an egg but not a newspaper, and sound travelling along a flashlight beam.

The company also hit the 1,000,000-mark in 1938, a milestone widely bally-hooed in the press and movie-house newsreels. yet GM was still hurting and it took World War Two to give the company new life.

The war triggered expansion for GM in Windsor and, in

The degree to which working conditions have changed over the years is dramatically illustrated in these two photos of GM employees on the job. The photo above, taken in 1940, shows workers assembling an endless stream of engines as GM boosted its wartime production to meet Canadian military needs. Below, an overall view of the bright and airy Lauzon Road GM trim plant.

The automotive industry's economic impact on Southwestern Ontario is measured, not just in the volume of vehicular and parts production, but also in the billions of dollars spent on new construction and expansion over the years. This scene shows construction crews working on one part of the assembly area of the General Motors Transmission Plant on Walker Road in the 1960s.

GENERAL MOTORS ARCHIVES

1940, the firm took over management of Border Cities Industries on Kildare Road near Walker, on what was known as Automobile Row. Windsor GM produced thousands of Browning submachine guns, engines for military aircraft, automatic rifles and naval gun mounts.

At war's end, the machine gun plant was sold to the city's bus company only to be repurchased by GM in 1978 when it became the Windsor Transmission plant — a $1-billion expansion.

GM returned to civilian production faster than its competitors, but not until 1950 did it reached 80,000 cars. That same year, GM released its 2,000,000th unit.

During the 1950s, the Walker Road plant produced engines, supplying the company's Canadian assembly lines as well as exporting to 10 other countries.

By 1955, the union and company were at loggerheads, leading to a 148-day strike affecting 1,000 hourly-rated employees in Windsor — about five per cent of GM's total workforce in Ontario. The strike came 11 months after the start of a long walkout at Ford. GM workers wanted higher wages to be on par with colleagues at other plants.

Their placards read:

"Get out of the wheat fields, GM, you're going against the grain."

and:

"We need more dough for the same old bread."

Workers lost about $1,600,000 before voting 87 percent in favour of the new terms.

In 1957, leadership at the Windsor plant changed. Manager

Although General Motors did not play a major role as car builder in Windsor, throughout the years it has had a strong presence as a parts and trim manufacturer. Above is the original Windsor GM Administration Building on Walker Road at Seminole, which came down in 1980 to make way for the new transmission building.

Below: The GM Trim Plant on Lauzon Road proudly displays its huge banner, boasting its Total Quality Category award.

D. K. MacDonald retired and was replaced by Philip A. Rudge. GM was producing 150,000 Chevrolet and Pontiac engines a year at its Walker Road plant. It was pumping $10,000,000 into Windsor's economy and Windsor workers were grossing $4,500,000 a year.

In the early '60s, GM enjoyed unprecedented sales but it still had to economize. Rumours persisted that the company was leaving Windsor. Engine blocks were cast at St. Catharines, then shipped to Windsor for machining, then shipped to Oshawa. It made more sense to produce the whole unit in St. Catharines and so, in 1963, GM moved its engine production there and converted the Windsor plant to automatic transmissions. It was taken over by McKinnon Industries of St. Catharines, a GM affiliate.

It was one of the most massive moves in Canadian auto history. Thousands of tons of machinery transferred between points 240 miles apart without disrupting production schedules. The entire procedure had to be finished by August, 1964 for the start-up of the '65 models. Huge mockups of the plants were built and machines tagged and moved. When one piece left Windsor, a counterpart left St. Catharines.

During the switch, the GM name temporarily vanished from Windsor as transmissions were produced by McKinnon.

The year 1965 was a banner one for the auto industry in Canada generally, and GM in particular. The company built its second plant in Windsor, a $20,000,000 trim plant on Lauzon Road. It was the largest single expansion in GM's history and a direct result of the Canada-U.S. Autopact.

Based on projections that car production would increase from 650,000 to 850,000 by 1970, it was a big boost for Windsor. The plant employed 1,700 workers — mostly women — cutting and sewing interior trim material for door panels, visors, seat covers and carpets.

E. H. (Ted) Taylor, president of GM said the plant was located in Windsor because of its skilled workforce, and to be close to the supply companies.

The new plant marked a progressive era in GM manage-

Nancy Novosel, Windsor GM Trim Plant worker, is shown cutting Trilaminate, a material used in Suzuki Side-Kicks, built in Ingersoll.

ment. The average age of the corporate executive was only 39. The building itself was a vast expanse of ultra-modern, shaded glass and contrasting white facing, earning it the nickname "The GM Hilton". There was even a quality control station inside that looked like a hotel registration desk.

Plant manager A. G. (Grant) Warner remembers the start-up of the plant: moving into the first office with temporary desks of plywood sheets on saw horses; paying the first hourly payroll in cash; getting a call from Colonel R. S. McLaughlin in Oshawa, who asked, "How are you young fellas making out down there?"

When it opened on November 25, 1965, the doors were draped in auto fabric and officials cut through it, instead of the traditional ribbon.

In 1969, GM reorganized its Canadian divisions and took over McKinnon industries, putting its logo on the Walker Road transmission operation. Renovations cost $1 billion, but it allowed GM to produce more than 4,000 transmissions a year in Windsor.

One year later the UAW struck GM in both Canada and the U.S., the first time both countries went out together. It was a calculated, expensive risk for the union. The strike lasted 67 days in the U.S. and 95 in Canada. The drain on the strike fund almost crippled the union.

It was a bitter dispute. Workers demanded that a cap on the Cost of Living Allowance (COLA) be lifted so their incomes would rise with inflation. Despite going to the brink, the union eventually won.

• • •

Mr. Sam was still Chairman of the Board at GM Canada. At 98 years old he visited the Oshawa office daily to, as he said, "keep an eye on things...".

Celebrating his 100th birthday in 1971, Oshawa and GM organized a parade of McLaughlin and McLaughlin-Buick cars — one for every year of production.

The parade wound through the city, past Mr. Sam and his family at their Parkwood Estate in Oshawa.

Mr. Sam's only comment on the news that night was a teasingly gruff:

"I made 'em all."

On January 6, 1972, Mr. Sam... The Colonel — Mister General Motors — died in his sleep.

Part Two:
The Challengers

A Part of Factory District, Windsor, Canada.

Ever wonder about the origin of the word "car"?

Webster's Third International Dictionary provides two historical roots:

1 — From Middle English carre, through the Ancient French carra, borrowed from a Latin word that meant vehicle.

2 — From carrus, of Celtic origin akin to Old Irish and Medieval Welsh, carr.

Take your pick, they all meant vehicle.

Webster's first definition for car is "a vehicle moving on wheels". A: "Archaic use for carriage, cart or wagon." D: "Automobile, especially private passenger automobile, as distinguished from a bus or truck."

It goes on, but the point is that, regardless of whether you call it bus, truck, automobile or just plain "car", Windsor has built them all.

Small Sparks In The Shadow Of The Big Three

hen we think of the auto industry in Windsor, we think of a powerful triumvirate: the Big Three — GM, Ford and Chrysler. They've maintained a presence in this city throughout most of the century — the survivors in this volatile and unpredictable industry.

Of the three, only Chrysler still produces vehicles in Windsor, its famous mini-van. Ford built cars here for 50 years, while GM only lasted a couple. All remain heavily involved with parts production, building engines, transmissions and automotive trim.

The Big Three are major employers and holders of real estate, making up a large part of the city's industrial district. Their presence is responsible for dozens of parts and associated supply industries. The Big Three loom so large in Windsor's manufacturing history that they overshadow two dozen lesser known car makers who fought for a share of the market.

Studebaker, for instance, was, at one point, second only to Ford. It's a name that ranks in stature with Pierce Arrow, Packard and Hupmobile.

But there were many other, less familiar companies living in the shadow of the giants. They lasted a year-or-two — or 20 — desperately trying to carve a niche, struggling to survive. Names like Gotfredson, Seagrave, Reo and Gramm have disappeared from the automotive lexicon.

Most of these companies were American branch plants, but a few were uniquely Canadian. The most successful was Menard, a small carriage-company-turned-car-maker, that never quite achieved its bright aspirations.

Regardless of their success or failure, each of these companies in its own way, helped to make Windsor the city that it is today, and so, deserves honourable mention.

CARL MORGAN COLLECTION

The LeBel Building, now the University of Windsor's School of Visual Arts, was originally intended as the site of a Packard assembly plant. See page 63.

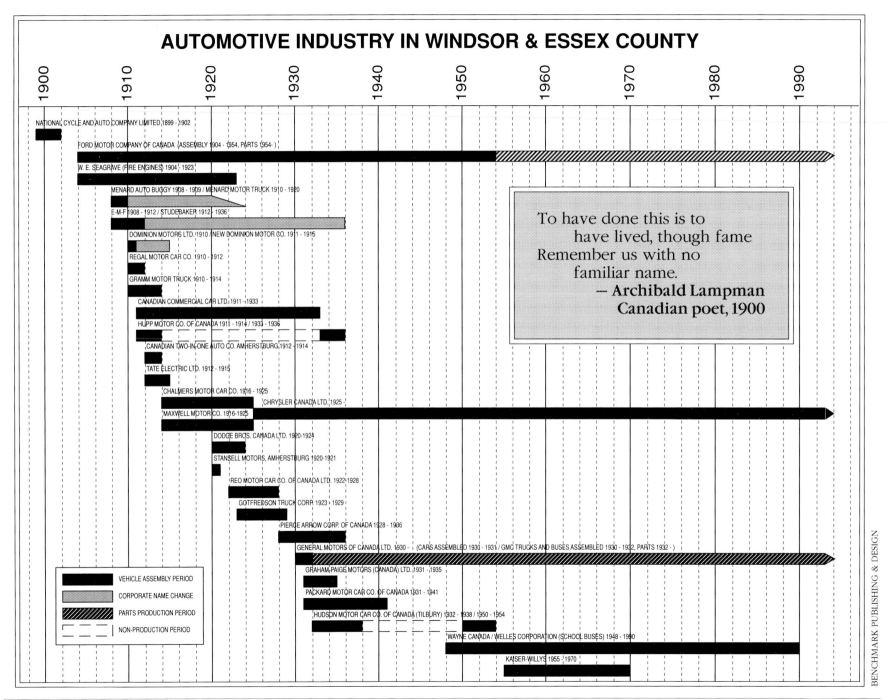

AUTOMOTIVE INDUSTRY IN WINDSOR & ESSEX COUNTY

1900 1910 1920 1930 1940 1950 1960 1970 1980 1990

NATIONAL CYCLE AND AUTO COMPANY LIMITED 1899 - 1902

FORD MOTOR COMPANY OF CANADA (ASSEMBLY 1904 - 1954, PARTS 1954-)

W. E. SEAGRAVE (FIRE ENGINES) 1904 - 1923

MENARD AUTO BUGGY 1908 - 1909 / MENARD MOTOR TRUCK 1910 - 1920

E-M-F 1908 - 1912 / STUDEBAKER 1912 - 1936

DOMINION MOTORS LTD. 1910 / NEW DOMINION MOTOR CO. 1911 - 1915

REGAL MOTOR CAR CO. 1910 - 1912

GRAMM MOTOR TRUCK 1910 - 1914

CANADIAN COMMERCIAL CAR LTD. 1911 - 1933

HUPP MOTOR CO. OF CANADA 1911 - 1914 / 1933 - 1936

CANADIAN TWO-IN-ONE AUTO CO. AMHERSTBURG 1912 - 1914

TATE ELECTRIC LTD. 1912 - 1915

CHALMERS MOTOR CAR CO. 1916 - 1925

CHRYSLER CANADA LTD. 1925 -

MAXWELL MOTOR CO. 1916-1925

DODGE BROS. CANADA LTD. 1920-1924

STANSELL MOTORS, AMHERSTBURG 1920-1921

REO MOTOR CAR CO. OF CANADA LTD. 1922-1928

GOTFREDSON TRUCK CORP. 1923 - 1929

PIERCE ARROW CORP. OF CANADA 1928 - 1936

GENERAL MOTORS OF CANADA LTD. 1930 - (CARS ASSEMBLED 1930 - 1931 / GMC TRUCKS AND BUSES ASSEMBLED 1930 - 1932, PARTS 1932 -)

GRAHAM-PAIGE MOTORS (CANADA) LTD. 1931 - 1935

PACKARD MOTOR CAR CO. OF CANADA 1931 - 1941

HUDSON MOTOR CAR CO. OF CANADA (TILBURY) 1932 - 1938 / 1950 - 1954

WAYNE CANADA / WELLES CORPORATION (SCHOOL BUSES) 1948 - 1990

KAISER-WILLYS 1955 - 1970

To have done this is to
have lived, though fame
Remember us with no
familiar name.
— Archibald Lampman
Canadian poet, 1900

VEHICLE ASSEMBLY PERIOD

CORPORATE NAME CHANGE

PARTS PRODUCTION PERIOD

NON-PRODUCTION PERIOD

BENCHMARK PUBLISHING & DESIGN

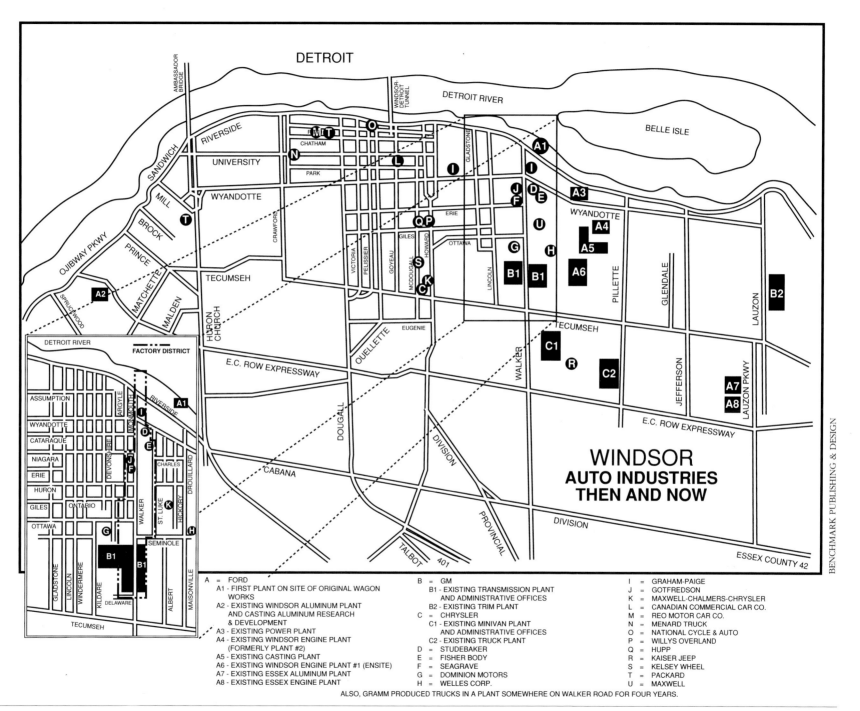

DETROIT

DETROIT RIVER

BELLE ISLE

**WINDSOR
AUTO INDUSTRIES
THEN AND NOW**

A = FORD
A1 - FIRST PLANT ON SITE OF ORIGINAL WAGON
        WORKS
A2 - EXISTING WINDSOR ALUMINUM PLANT
        AND CASTING ALUMINUM RESEARCH
        & DEVELOPMENT
A3 - EXISTING POWER PLANT
A4 - EXISTING WINDSOR ENGINE PLANT
        (FORMERLY PLANT #2)
A5 - EXISTING CASTING PLANT
A6 - EXISTING WINDSOR ENGINE PLANT #1 (ENSITE)
A7 - EXISTING ESSEX ALUMINUM PLANT
A8 - EXISTING ESSEX ENGINE PLANT

B = GM
B1 - EXISTING TRANSMISSION PLANT
        AND ADMINISTRATIVE OFFICES
B2 - EXISTING TRIM PLANT
C = CHRYSLER
C1 - EXISTING MINIVAN PLANT
        AND ADMINISTRATIVE OFFICES
C2 - EXISTING TRUCK PLANT
D = STUDEBAKER
E = FISHER BODY
F = SEAGRAVE
G = DOMINION MOTORS
H = WELLES CORP.

I = GRAHAM-PAIGE
J = GOTFREDSON
K = MAXWELL-CHALMERS-CHRYSLER
L = CANADIAN COMMERCIAL CAR CO.
M = REO MOTOR CAR CO.
N = MENARD TRUCK
O = NATIONAL CYCLE & AUTO
P = WILLYS OVERLAND
Q = HUPP
R = KAISER JEEP
S = KELSEY WHEEL
T = PACKARD
U = MAXWELL

ALSO, GRAMM PRODUCED TRUCKS IN A PLANT SOMEWHERE ON WALKER ROAD FOR FOUR YEARS.

"Mose" L. Menard:
Self-Proclaimed Father Of The Canadian Car

Moise or "Mose" L. Menard, a tough, successful, shrewd blacksmith-turned-automaker had a dream. He wanted his name, like Henry Ford's, to become a household word.

Menard didn't quite reach that goal, even though he was good at what he did. The Menard Auto Buggy Company flourished from 1908 to 1920 under different names including Menard Commercial Car Company and Menard Motor Company of Windsor.

"Mose" was born August 13, 1859 in Belle River. He left school at 14 to work in his father's blacksmith shop where he shod horses and worked metal for two years before apprenticing with Alfred Pulford, a wagon-maker from Ruthven.

Although born into a family of modest means, Menard's fortunes improved when he bought two boxcar loads of binder twine at 5 1/2 cents a pound and parlayed it into $10,000 when the Spanish-American war broke out, pushing the value of the twine to 23 cents a pound.

In 1902, with money to spare, he launched Menard's Windsor Carriage and Delivery Wagon Works, quickly becoming the largest wagon dealer in the county.

Menard dabbled with the internal combustion engine and realized the automobile was here to stay. He asked a Detroit engineer to design a car which he began producing in 1908, from his factory at 100 London Street West (University Avenue) at Caron.

A husky, tough-minded blacksmith, Menard called himself The Father of the Canadian Car. He claimed to be "the first to advertise Windsor-made motor products and the first to demonstrate the potential of Windsor as an automotive centre."

He called his cars "Autobuggies". They were crude, but solidly built, and ran well. The first had a traditional buggy

Moise "Mose" Menard called his cars "Auto-buggies"

WINDSOR STAR LIBRARY

seat and huge wheels for manoeuvring rutted country roads.

The Autobuggy was popular on the Prairies and in Quebec but, by 1910, the market softened as tastes changed. Buyers no longer wanted high-wheelers, as Menard's buggy-like cars, were called.

Knowing he had to shift with the times, Menard designed a vehicle with a water-cooled engine. He was one of the first Canadians to show at the Toronto Exhibition and trade shows in Montreal and London.

Menard, under pressure from Ford, switched to trucks, believing the business world would be the chief buyers. Years later, he recognized his mistake — he had moved too soon.

The Menard Motor Truck Company was one of the first to build a six-cylinder engine. By 1913, he had a full range of

1908-09: The Walkerville Fire Department used a Menard truck chassis and equipped it with fire-fighting chemicals.

trucks and, during World War One, shipped some to France.

In 1916, Menard built a fire truck with an aerial ladder, one of three Menard trucks used by the Walkerville Fire Department over the next 20 years. He also made the first street washer in Windsor.

In 1920, after 46 years in business, Menard sold his company to Maple Leaf Motors, a manufacturing firm based in Montreal — but the company was gone within a few years.

As for Menard, he was financially comfortable and continued his career in politics, He held office at the town and county levels, and by 1923, he was mayor of Riverside. He died in 1946 at 87.

1917: Bell Telephone service truck was built by Menard Motor Truck Company

The Challengers

Included in the array of specialized firefighting equipment manufactured by Seagrave was this horse-drawn rig, equipped with runners, for winter use. It was sold to the fire department at Three Rivers, Quebec.

This red brick building in the 900-block of Walker Road was the home of Seagrave Fire Apparatus Company in the early 1900s.

The body of Frederic S. Seagrave, founder of the Seagrave Fire Apparatus Company, Ohio, is interred in the family mausoleum at Windsor Grove Cemetery.

First With Fire Engines In Canada

Walkerville was home to W. E. Seagrave Fire Apparatus Company, a subsidiary of an Ohio firm established in 1881. Owned by Warren E. Seagrave, it was the first fire engine maker in Canada and many of the early models were horse-drawn.

Seagrave opened on Walker Road in 1904 and delivered three Seagrave motor fire engines to Vancouver in 1907 — the first of hundreds turned out for fire departments across Canada.

In 1910, Windsor bought an aerial truck and in 1914, replaced its horse-drawn steamer with a motor-powered pumper which wasn't scrapped until 1947.

London also bought a Seagrave combination truck. Although heavily damaged in a train collision in 1913, the fire department thought so highly of the vehicle that, instead of scrapping it, the truck was sent to Walkerville to be rebuilt.

For 16 years, Seagrave produced air- and water-cooled fire engines but found himself in financial trouble when rival American-LaFrance set up in Toronto in 1915.

To save his company, Seagrave tried merging with Loughead Machine Company in Sarnia, to produce a line of heavy-duty trucks. The move failed and the company locked its doors in 1923.

Top: Windsor's first motorized pumper built in 1914 by Seagrave, was known as "Old Mike". It was scrapped in 1947.

Lower right: They may have been breaking some kind of law, but this pyramid of men caused quite a stir riding in a 1914 Seagrave pumper through Windsor streets.

Lower left: Frederic Seagrave (far right) was on hand, along with his son, Warren, in 1911 when the Ottawa Fire Department took delivery of its first motorized fire engine.

The Challengers

Top: Studebaker's presence in Windsor was somewhat convoluted almost from the day it took over the E-M-F Company, which was then manufacturing cars in the former Globe Furniture Company on Montreuil Street.

Bottom left: Although Studebaker continued car production in the former furniture factory, its offices were at 530 Walker Road, later the home of Standard Printing until 1993.

Bottom right: At one time, Studebaker was second only to Ford in car production and employment, and to keep up with growing customer demand, the company built a new assembly plant. Although this artist's conception exaggerates the dimensions, it was a substantial building in Windsor's "Factory District".

Studebaker And The E-M-F

Studebaker, with its distinctive, futuristic, post-war styling, was one of the more romantic names in the auto industry. Ahead of its time, it was popular with car buffs for its get-up-and-go.

The Studebaker was always a classy looking car and Canadians were fonder of them than were the Americans. In fact, Studebaker was in business in Canada three years longer than in the U.S. and, at one point, was second only to Ford in employment and output in Windsor.

Its Windsor roots trace back to 1908-09 when an American firm called the E-M-F Company bought the Globe Furniture Factory on Montreuil Road to produce the E-M-F 30 and Flanders 20. It was one of the busiest car plants in Windsor.

Although local wags claimed the name E-M-F stood for "Every Mechanical Failure and Every Morning Fix-it", in reality, it came from the first initial of the last name of its three

Pioneering The Auto Age

founders: Barney F. Everett, William A. Metzger and the real genius — Walter E. Flanders. All three had been involved in the industry for some time. Metzger was a sales manager for Cadillac, Everett made auto trim, and Flanders was an automotive engineer who liked expensive, finely finished cars.

Originally from the hay fields of Vermont, Flanders was an outspoken industrialist who often clashed with Ford. He was a big, burly, rough-mannered man with a large head and shock of bristling hair. He liked strong cigars and drink. He died at 52 in Virginia in 1923 — ironically, from injuries suffered in an automobile accident.

Using Canadian capital, E-M-F built its first cars in 1910. The humble Flanders was well-received, featuring right hand drive, an open front and big brass headlights, fuelled by acetylene tanks. A solid, peppy performer, it could reach speeds of 45 miles an hour.

The E-M-F, on the other hand, was dogged by trouble and generally disliked. Two years after the launch, a dispute erupted between E-M-F and Studebaker, the company's American distributor. The dispute was settled and led to takeover of E-M-F by Studebaker — which found itself thrust into the Canadian manufacturing scene.

The Studebaker Corporation of Canada offices were at 530 Walker Road, the building which later housed Standard Printing. Flanders became vice-president and continued producing E-M-F cars until 1912, when they were renamed Studebaker 20 and 30.

Studebaker had a long history as a carriage maker in the U.S. The company was founded in the U.S. in 1852 by brothers Clement and Henry and was known for its Prairie Schooner and Conestoga wagons. Its first car, an electric, appeared in 1902.

In 1913, Studebaker introduced a successful line of five cars

Believe it or not, the first vehicles produced by brothers Studebaker were Prairie Schooners and Conestoga Wagons (above). In a later step up, the company produced the Runabout with a stick seat and no top (below).

Above: 1929 Studebaker in front of the gates to Willistead Manor.

Right: *Studebaker employees work on the body trim line of the 1934 model.*

ranging from $900 to $1,800. More than 3,000 were built the first year and Studebaker's popularity continued for the next 15.

The company's advertising boasted: "Press a button and the brilliant electric headlights illuminate the road." The days of oil and acetylene headlights were over.

During Prohibition, Studebaker's seven-passenger E.K. Big Six was a favourite of rum-runners. With the back seat out, it could carry 50 gallon jugs. Referred to as the Whiskey Six, the car could rev up to 80 miles an hour. The $3,000 price tag was chalked up as the cost of doing business.

In 1921, the Windsor Police Department bought its own Studebaker chase car — though they called it the Police Flyer instead of a Whiskey Six.

Generally, Packards, Cadillacs and Lincolns were used to run booze. One of the most unusual belonged to the notorious Al Capone who frequented the Border Towns. His made-to-order car was a 1928 bullet-proof Cadillac protected by half-inch boiler plate and inch-thick glass. The gas tank was shielded by sheet steel and the car was equipped with a siren and secret gun lockers. It also had a roll-down rear window.

Studebaker suffered its first major setback in 1927 when it gambled on the lower-priced Erskine, named after company president, Albert A. Erskine.

More trouble followed when Studebaker united with Pierce-Arrow. The company set up a distribution/sales office in Walkerville in 1928 and a small number were actually assembled. Trouble was, Pierce-Arrow had been in financial straits for 10 years, even though it was a car of distinction, the choice of kings and sultans. The most expensive model in the U.S. was sold to Persian Shah Riza Khan, who ordered a gold radiator and diamond studded convertible top. The price: a cool $25,000.

Always noted for its distinctive, classy styling, Studebaker enjoyed popularity among Canadians. In 1913 it introduced a successful line of five models, including this convertible sedan. Prices ranged from $900 to $1,800.

Studebaker Gave Birth To IAC

Studebaker was an innovator in many ways. In 1925, the company set up a loans office — a small, two-person corner office in the Studebaker building in Walkerville. It provided car loans at a time when most purchases were cash only and few companies were willing to provide credit.

From those modest beginnings in Windsor, the business grew into the Industrial Acceptance Corporation, a separate entity that expanded rapidly to become Canada's largest finance company.

The IAC became a leader in industrial, commercial, real estate and corporate financing with assets over $3 billion. In 1979, it became the Continental Bank of Canada, this country's 12th largest bank.

Pierce Arrow, founded by Richard Pierce, of Buffalo, N.Y. was a leader in its day. Its name conjured images of speed, luxury and elegance. Its advanced engineering included a gear shift on the steering column. Unfortunately the company lacked new ideas after World War One and fell behind. It dropped its prices, but it was too little, too late.

When the Depression hit, Pierce Arrow went begging for buyers. Instead of producing a smaller, cheaper car, the company stuck with the expensive 8 and 12-cylinder gas-guzzlers. By 1933 the parent firm was in receivership.

Instead of hunkering down and riding out the economic storm, the U.S. firm offered no fewer than 47 body designs. By 1936, a sharp cut in protective Canadian tariffs and reorgani-zation of the American firm ended with the Canadian plant closing. A sales office remained but the cars came from the U.S.

The next year, after dropping prices as low as $700 without buyer response, the company folded.

In 1939, with the introduction of the low-priced Studebaker "Champion", there was talk of reopening the Canadian plant in Windsor but the war intervened. The company didn't make a comeback until 1949, working out of a former munitions plant in Hamilton.

Try as it might, it couldn't match the competition and closed in South Bend, Indiana, in 1963 and in Hamilton in March, 1966.

If your present car runs as well as it looks, you can own the Packard pictured on this card with *no additional down payment* and only $ a month to pay. Drop in today and let us figure out a deal for you.

Gordon W. Edwards, Ltd
Packard Division
Corner Chatham and Church Sts
Windsor

Mr. Thos. Ferry.
112 Louis Ave
City

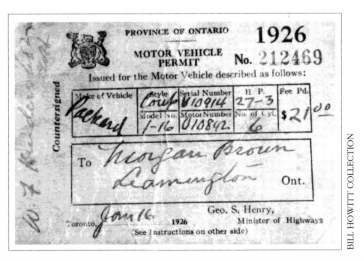

Packard — A Car For The World's Elite

As the automobile industry matured, car owners represented a cross-section of the community that wasn't much different from today. Everyone from doctors to lawyers, bankers, merchants, factory workers, housewives and farmers wanted to own a car.

Some were rich, others were not. They were single, married, with families and without, but they had two things in common: optimism and large dollops of faith, which helped them cope with balky automobiles that were prone to frequent breakdowns.

While most people endured, James Ward Packard did not. Around the turn of the century, he bought an early model and was so angry about its performance that he wrote a letter to the manufacturer:

"I got one of your damn cars. It's no good! I could make a better one myself..."

Putting his money where his mouth was, he produced one of the finest automobiles of its day. Boasting that his motor carriage was made for the critical patron, his advertising message was:

"Ask the man who owns one!"

Packard launched his business in the U.S. at the turn of the century when he got three orders for cars at the New York Auto Show. At the time, few expected a car — made with crudely machined parts — to run dependably. The Packard was different. It was a powerful, heavy, well-built machine with distinctive hub caps and radiator. Body changes were infrequent and advertising boasted that the Packard remained new for 10 years.

By 1914, the U.S. Company was selling to the world's elite: the Czar of Russia owned one, as did a Maharaja in India and a Viscount in New Zealand.

Work in Windsor began in 1931 at Chatham and Church streets, where the Canadian Tire Company now stands. While sales dropped in the U.S., Canadian production under L. L.

Pioneering The Auto Age

This 1932 Convertible Victoria is one of five Packards owned by Windsor car collector Bill Howitt. It was built in Detroit, brought to Windsor in parts for assembly, then shipped to a customer in Victoria, British Columbia. It is a powerful car with a super eight engine, and features a vacuum-operated clutch.

BILL HOWITT COLLECTION

Roberts, the company's first Canadian manager, climbed to 500 cars a year and the company couldn't keep up with demand even during the Depression.

Windsor car collector Bill Howitt ran errands for Packard and remembers the company's main office at 40 Ouellette Avenue near the ferry docks next to the import-export office.

In 1933, the Windsor company moved to the 900 block of St. Luke Road, home of the old Fisher Body Building.

The first Windsor-made Packard rolled off the line draped with a Union Jack. Guests included Windsor Mayor David Croll, Packard President Alvan Macauley, Sandwich Mayor Joseph Donnelly and Hugh Graybiel, publisher of *The Windsor Star*. A reception was held at the Prince Edward Hotel where Macauley installed the hubcaps to complete the car.

Unfortunately for Packard, the vagaries of the auto industry caught up with him in 1935. Packard was a conservative car builder, and once he established a model, it remained unchanged for years. As competition increased, his sales faltered.

He tried winning back his market with a new V-8 engine and banked heavily on his reputation as a quality car builder. Twelve thousand orders poured in for the new car before it was even built, but the final product fell short of public expectations and sales dwindled.

Packard's car looked stubby and boxy while the public wanted a touch of flash at an affordable price. Although the signals were there, Packard hung on. Production peaked in 1937 with 2,500 cars in Canada. That turned out to be an aberration as customers refused to accept hold-overs from another era.

In 1941, Packard turned his Windsor plant over to the military and, in '44 started work on a new building on Huron Church Road, between College and Millen. It is now the University of Windsor's LeBel Building.

General Manager F. G. Williams planned to sell lower priced cars to boost sales. His new building was built as an assembly plant but was used as a parts warehouse for the 200 Canadian Packard dealers.

Conditions deteriorated and by 1958, Packard shut down.

The Welles Corporation, which manufactured as many as 1,000 school buses a year, was dogged by bad luck. In May 1986, fire destroyed the sheet metal shop and much of the assembly line operation.

Warford — Wayne — Welles

Anyone living in Windsor before 1990 will remember the school bus chassis stacked along Riverside Drive in Walkerville. No seats, box, doors or windows — just orange engine mounts connected to a steering wheel, and a black painted chassis on wheels.

The buses were built by Wayne Canada (Welles Manufacturing Limited), the largest bus maker in Ontario. In 1925, the Warford Corporation of Canada was launched in Windsor. It would become one of the longest-surviving auto companies in the city.

Warford started as an auto accessories firm headed by Halsey C. Welles, and grew into a major manufacturer of specialty vehicles including parcel delivery truck bodies.

Bus production began in 1948 when the company became the Welles Corporation and turned out more school buses than any Canadian company — averaging 200 bodies a year. Engines were provided by the Big Three.

By the mid-'80s, Welles built 1,000 buses a year at its Metcalfe Street plant, shipping across Canada until disaster struck in May 1986.

Jean Cote, a Welles employee, was bicycling to work when he saw smoke rising in the distance — the plant was burning. The fire broke out at 3 a.m. and two teenagers, seen leaving the scene, were suspected of arson.

Flames rose five stories and smoke was visible in the town of Essex, 20 miles distant. The sheet metal shop and half of the assembly lines, as well as 38 buses, were destroyed.

For Cote, then 58, it was his third strike. He had stayed in Windsor when Ford moved to Oakville, then lost his job at Bendix when that company moved out. He had hoped to retire from Welles. Suddenly, like so many others, he was in danger of becoming another unemployed statistic — too young to pack it in, too old to find something new.

• • •

The company moved to temporary quarters — four garage bays on Sprucewood in West Windsor where 22 of the 228 employees assembled the remaining 115 vehicles. Plans were started to get the company on its feet. Local politicians and the union appealed for government aid when the company said it would rebuild in Canada.

The Ontario Development Corporation granted a $1,000,000 loan and the city bought the old site for $250,000. The company moved into new quarters on Marentette in the empty Sheller Globe building, a steering wheel manufacturer that had closed. Two hundred and twelve days after the fire, 600 people watched the first bus roll off the new line. The employees were reinstated with plans to build 1,800 new vehicles.

It never happened.

By October, 1989 Welles hinted at layoffs. School boards cut their budgets and the market dropped 30 per cent. The following April, workers were told the company was closing.

Welles was bought by Richmond Transportation corporation of Richmond, Indiana, and despite signs of fresh optimism, the company eventually closed the doors, packed up and left.

• • •

Cote couldn't find work after July, 1990, and decided to retire on his Canada Pension. By spring 1993, he had not found other work. He said he received no severance pay, though he was to begin receiving $5.50 a month from the Ontario Pension Fund for his time at Welles.

In 1990, after getting back on its feet with support from the city and provincial governments, the plant was closed.

Upper right: This 1928 photo was taken at Walkerville Number 2 Firehall at Turner and Tecumseh roads. The fire engine body was built by Gotfredson-Bickle in Walkerville. The fire chief's car at left is a 1920s Studebaker.

Lower right: A Gotfredson truck was converted into a passenger bus and ran between Windsor and Belle River.

Gotfredson Built A Name In Trucks

The name Gotfredson doesn't roll off the tongue with the easy familiarity of Ford or Chrysler, but the company became one of the major truck manufacturers in North America! Gotfredson built medium and heavy trucks with a reputation for a distinctive, highly-polished cast-aluminum radiator shell. They sold coast-to-coast, advertised as "The best truck in the world."

In 1923, Gotfredson-Joyce Incorporated produced a truck called the "G and J". Two years later the firm was reorganized as Gotfredson Truck Corporation, merging with American Auto Trimming Company Limited, a Walkerville parts supply company established in 1911 by Benjamin Gotfredson of Detroit.

During World War One, Gotfredson produced gun carriers and army trucks. Later, it manufactured buses, taxis, fire engine chassis and passenger car bodies for Studebaker. The company became a major supplier of parts and truck bodies for Ford, and a distributor of diesel engines. It employed more than 400 men and women at its peak. Frank J. Mitchell, Windsor mayor from 1924 to 1926, was sales manager for the company.

In 1925, Windsor Police bought a Gotfredson truck for use as a patrol wagon.

Gotfredson was more popular in Canada, where production reached 2,000 units a year, well ahead of the U.S. Although the Canadian operation outlived its American counterpart, it ran into money problems and bankruptcy proceedings were started in 1929. Studebaker rented the buildings, hired the 110-man staff and took over production of Erskine and Studebaker bodies.

The company continued building auto bodies and parts until the 1960s, long after truck manufacturing ended. The final vestiges of Gotfredson in Windsor disappeared on Canada Day in 1985 when two large buildings on Walker Road at Niagara Street burned. One of them had been occupied by Gotfredson.

WINDSOR POLICE SERVICES

One of the Windsor Police Department's early automotive purchases was this Gotfredson-built patrol wagon.

FRANÇOIS BABY HOUSE MUSEUM

American Auto Trimming of Walkerville (right) merged with Gotfredson-Joyce in 1925 to become Gotfredson Truck Corporation, a major Walkerville manufacturer of distinctive Canadian trucks.

The Challengers

Jeep Rides To The Rescue

If you were in Windsor in February, 1965, and remember the 30-inch snowfall that paralyzed Essex County — you might remember Kaiser Jeep of Canada riding to the rescue. Kaiser employees picked up stranded motorists, delivered insulin to diabetics, meals to the elderly and took expectant mothers and accident victims to hospital.

The snow fell for two days. Highways were closed, the Ontario Provincial Police were snowbound, hundreds of people were stranded, and storm equipment was overtaxed. It was the worst storm in 21 years.

Enter Kaiser Jeep.

The company stopped production and mobilized a quasi-military operation, responding to more than half of the 700 distress calls it received. The four-wheel-drive vehicles went where others couldn't.

Under the direction of H. Gordon Munro, Kaiser's general manager, office employees staffed the phones while plant workers drove 30 vehicles on mercy missions.

In one dramatic incident, James Pierson, a Jeep driver, discovered an ambulance stuck near the Canadian Salt Company. The radio was dead and the crew had been there eight hours. It took two hours to tow the ambulance to safety.

• • •

Kaiser-Willys of Canada Limited was one of the last of the smaller auto companies to make a go of it in Windsor. Its Canadian presence began in 1914 when Willys Overland set up in Hamilton and then Toronto. The company was a branch plant of an American firm owned by John North Willys, a sporting goods dealer.

Until 1926, car bodies were supplied by Canadian Top and Body of Tilbury. The company evolved into an assembly plant for Hudson Motor Car Company and then Hudson-Essex and Hudson-Nash, building Canadian Hudson products until 1954.

In 1934 Willys Overland opened its Canadian headquarters at 318 Giles Blvd., East, next to the Hupp plant. The Windsor

1965: A Jeep threads its way through snow-blocked Windsor streets to help hundreds of stranded motorists.

City Directory lists the company until 1940, though it's doubtful that any production took place in Windsor. Canadian production began and ended in 1934 and cars were imported from the U.S. after that.

Kaiser-Willys was formed in 1953, when American industrialist Henry Kaiser took over the Willys organization. In 1955, Kaiser Jeep of Canada Limited, assembled jeeps at 2525 Central Avenue as a subsidiary of Kaiser Jeep of Toledo, Ohio. It was the only manufacturer of four-wheel-drive utility vehicles in Canada.

"Jeep" comes from the initials G.P. (general-purpose vehicle) used in World War Two. The first Windsor-made Jeep came off the line at the Central Avenue plant in August, 1959.

In 1967, the company won a $2,800,000 government contract for 800 military jeeps for the Canadian Armed Forces. Production reached 2,700, including the Gladiator and Jeep C.J. with parts from Toledo.

Kaiser's presence in Windsor was short. Production dropped below 1,000. In 1970 it was taken over by American Motors and the Windsor plant closed.

Dodge Brothers Came in 1892

John and Horace E. Dodge had an on-again-off-again relationship with Windsor beginning in 1892, the year that Windsor became a city.

At the time they worked for the Canadian Typograph Company which later became the National Cycle and Auto Company. George H. Thompson, a shipping clerk at the Windsor factory recalls the brothers applying for work and being told by the superintendent that only one was needed. John said they had always worked together and if both weren't hired, neither would start.

They were hired and John soon became superintendent.

The two redheads were hard-working, hard-drinking, tough businessmen and master machinists. They ignored all correspondence not addressed to both, and even capitalized the "B" in "brothers" as if it were a proper name.

The Dodge boys took over the company in 1900 and built Evans and Dodge chainless bicycles. The shop was at the top of Ferry Hill on Ouellette Avenue, leading down to the riverfront ferry landing.

When they sold the company at the end of the first year, the new management wanted John to stay on at their Hamilton plant, but he refused to budge without his brother. They moved back to Detroit, where they set up their own shop to make transmissions for Olds Motor Works.

In 1903, Henry Ford offered them each 50 shares in his new company if they'd build engines for him. They ignored the warnings of friends who figured Ford wouldn't last long and bought $20,000 worth of stock — or 10 per cent of the Ford Motor Company — returning a cool $25,000,000 in 1919.

Ford criticized them for paying piece-work, a common practice at the time, but one that Ford felt led to poor quality. They sensed that Ford was on the verge of cutting them loose,

One of the line of Dodge Brothers trucks manufactured by Dodge Brothers of Canada Limited of Windsor-Walkerville in the 1920s. The company was founded by John and Horace Dodge.

so they left and founded their own company — Dodge Brothers Incorporated.

They planned to manufacture their own car, but fate intervened and, in 1920, within months of each other, they died of pulmonary pneumonia during a flu epidemic.

The Dodge name was back in Windsor in 1920 with a company called Dodge Brothers of Canada Limited of Windsor-Walkerville. It was a subsidiary of the Detroit Company and assembled Dodge vehicles from imported parts. In 1924, the company moved to larger quarters on Walker Road.

The Windsor connection was short-lived as the operation was shifted to Toronto where it built Dodge and Graham Brothers trucks until Chrysler absorbed it in 1928.

In 1929, Dodge Brothers production returned to Windsor with models bearing the Chrysler insignia. Dodge, Chrysler, Plymouth and Desoto models were produced at the new Chrysler plant in South Walkerville. The "Brothers" portion of the name was eliminated in 1933 when it became the "Dodge" division.

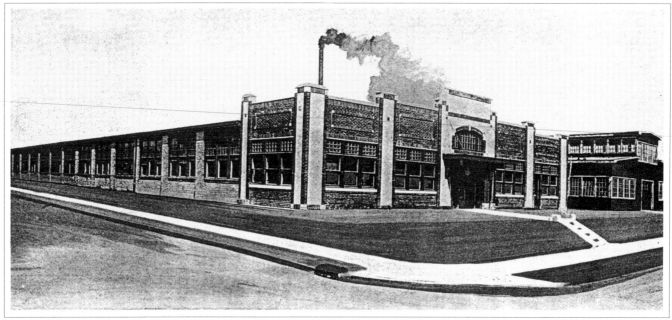

The Hupp Motor Car Company in Windsor started modestly in 1911. The Hupmobile, also known as the "Little Red Car", became so popular that the company moved to these new quarters at Giles and McDougall, where Electrozad Supply Company stands today.

FRANÇOIS BABY HOUSE MUSEUM

Optimism Was High In 1911 As Two New Companies Put Down Roots

The year 1911 gave birth to two companies that seemed to have promising futures.

Better known of the two was the Hupp Motor Car Company, founded by Robert Hupp, a Detroit engineer. The firm manufactured the famous Hupmobile or "Little Red Car", a low-slung angular machine with high-perched headlamps.

It sold for under $1,000 though the top, doors and acetylene lamps were extra. It was such a popular little car that the company outgrew its space at the Medway Power Building and moved to new quarters at Giles and McDougall.

Hupmobile was one of the first North American cars to use a pressed-steel body. By 1914, some models even came with full electrical equipment at no extra charge. It was advertised as "Guaranteed for Life".

Hupmobile production ended in 1914 when the firm retreated to the U.S. It returned to Canada between 1933 and 1936, and then imported cars again until 1941.

Canadian Commercial Motor Car

The second child of 1911 was the Canadian Commercial Motor Car Company Limited at 509 Goyeau Street. It was probably the first Canadian firm to manufacture only commercial vehicles. Included was a light delivery wagon called "The Canadian". It had a screened-in body and ebony steering wheel — all for $1,600. The company motto had an uncharacteristically patriotic ring:

"Deliver the Goods the Canadian way".

Records are unclear about the company's lifespan, but it may have been in business as late as 1933.

Hupmobile

Touring Car, regular equipment $ o.b. Windsor
With electric lighting and starting, demountable rims,
over-size tires, tire carrier $1180 f.o.b. Windsor.

The Car for the Farmer's Famil

re any *real reason* why the farmer should prefer the Hupmobile
ome other car?

re convinced that there are a *dozen such reasons.*

t every automobile maker tells you in a general way that you
ht to buy his car.

we want to go further—*we want to tell you why* we believe your
ice should be a Hupmobile.

re convinced, and we are sure you will convince yourself, that it
especially suited to the needs of a farmer's family.

f the prime reasons why it is so suited is the low cost of repairs.

nobile records for five years prove that *positively.*

show every dollar's worth of repair parts sold to dealers and
nsumers.

on an average mileage of 5,000 miles per year to each car, the
air cost per mile per car is so amazingly low as to be *almost
believable.*

nounts to 27 mills per mile—27 cents for every hundred miles.

s and figures on this subject will be sent you on application.

pmobile farmer almost invariably gets longer tire wear.

He gets it because Hupmobile solid steel construction i
construction.

The tires wear longer, moreover, because of the steady im
long-stroke engine—less snubbing and rubbing and
jolting.

That long-stroke engine alone is one of the dozen reasons f
Hupmobile in preference to any other car.

Another mighty practical reason is the *high price which th
commands* as a second-hand car.

People don't give more for a used Hupmobile than they
cars of the same price without sound, sensible reasons.

It's especially suited even to unimproved roads—becau
though staunch, and skims the rough places.

It's a family car because of these things—a farmer's
because it isn't a luxury but a downright saving.

It's good-looking. It's different. There isn't a cheap tl

We can—and will in other advertisements—give you otl
reasons.

But there are enough for one advertisement. Go to your
dealer and give him a chance to continue the story.

Hupp Motor Car Company, Desk N, Windsor, Ont.

A Few Hup "Whys"

center control—either side
front entrance.

ibrationless steering wheel

hort turning radius 40 ft

"Lively" motor—quick re-
sponse to throttle

ittle of customary motor
vibration

Dash control of hot and cold

Simple carburetor—no deli-
cate adjustments neces-
sary.

Certain clutch action

Simple, infallible oiling system.

Rain vision, ventilating
windshield

Quickly adjustable

Low center of gravity—good
looks, easy riding, few
skids, no turning over.

Gasoline tank under cowl,
nearly over carburetor
assuring constant flow of
gas.

All moving parts are
"Streamline" bo
now being adop
highest-priced car

Accessibility and I
in weight of start
tem.

*Alfred St. Louis, whose ancestors were among Windsor's early
settlers, owned a Hupmobile in 1927.*

*The Canadian Commercial Motor Car Company was one of
the first firms to manufacture only commercial vehicles,
including this light delivery wagon called "The Canadian".*

Amherstburg Tries Twice

The ill-fated Amherst 40, a five-seat "touring car", was designed so that it could be converted to a truck by removing the back seat and doors, and replacing them with a box.

In 1911 a group of Detroit promoters swept into Amherstburg looking for two things — a town ready to gamble on the future of the burgeoning auto industry — and local investors with money to risk.

These City Slickers arrived in a spanking new roadster — prototype of the kind they wanted to build. They convinced local politicians, and the editor of *The Amherstburg Echo* to back their scheme.

The Echo trumpeted:

"Don't knock, just boost. Be a doer. Let's get on the map with other Canadian towns going forward this year."

Amherstburg put up $25,000, expecting the Detroiters to do the same, providing seed money for the Canadian Two-In-One Automobile Company which opened in the former Pulford Carriage Shop at Simcoe and Sandwich Streets.

The first model was a car-truck combination called the Amherst 40. The five-seat passenger car could be converted to

a 1,500-pound truck by removing the buggy-style back seat and doors, replacing them with a box. Such conversions were common but the "Amherst 40" was the first touring car actually designed for it. Billed as "the car with a difference", it was a forerunner of the pickup truck.

The prototype pulled a dilapidated sight-seeing bus 20 miles over rough roads in less than an hour, and took five people to Windsor in about the same time.

For a while it appeared the company had potential. One car was displayed at the Toronto Exhibition and six others were in the works. However, by September the project was abandoned, even though a factory was built and machinery purchased. Local investors produced two more cars, but declared bankruptcy when they couldn't pay the U.S. suppliers. The company never moved into its one-storey, brick and concrete building at Fort and Sandwich streets where Faucher Lumber is today.

On February 12, 1915, shareholders met to wind up the company. The building and property were transferred to the town in lieu of a mortgage. The company's assets were auctioned. The father of local history buff David Botsford bought the frames, steering gears, rear axles, two radiators and two brass cut-out emblems. He intended to complete a car, but it never happened.

The three completed cars were sold to Colin Wigle, Alfred Woods and a well-known doctor, Frederick Park who drove his for several years. Dr. Park was also mayor of the town and a major backer of the company.

• • •

Five years later a similar venture surfaced when car salesman William Riley Stansell hit town. He was described as a valiant businessman, a solid-citizen and a persuasive promoter with a gift of the gab.

Stansell planned to build 10,000 cars a year. He convinced Amherstburg citizens to finance Stansell Motors and promised to reward them with a five-passenger touring car that would sell for $2,500.

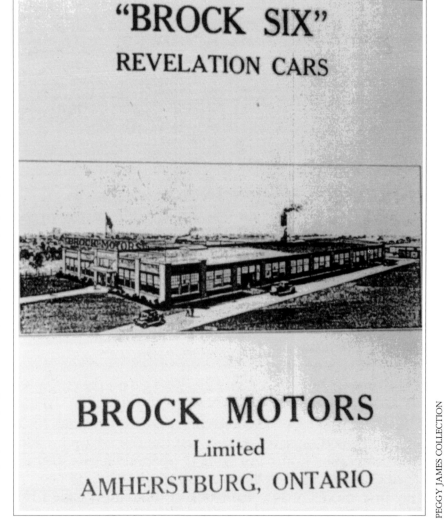

"BROCK SIX"
REVELATION CARS

BROCK MOTORS
Limited
AMHERSTBURG, ONTARIO

In the 1920s, Brock Motors was established in Amherstburg to produce a touring car known as the Brock Six. Only one was known to have been built before the company folded and the promoter left town.

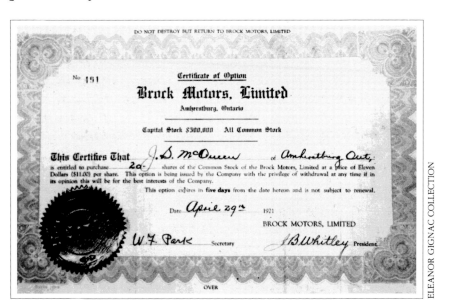

Dr. Frederick Park, Amherstburg's mayor at the time, was the proud owner of both an Amherst 40 and the one and only Brock Six.

He set up shop in the factory built for the ill-fated Amherst 40 but lack of money brought it to a quick end. The company was reorganized in 1921 as Brock Motors Limited — named after General Isaac Brock, Canada's hero of The War of 1812. The plan was to build a quiet, smooth-running car known as the "Brock Six", a large touring car.

The one car produced was bought by none other than Dr. Park, again one of the shareholders in the ill-fated firm.

A fan of self-propelled transport, Park also owned the first motor bike in Amherstburg, often making his rounds, slip-sliding through the mud and snow on rutted rural roads. He was an advocate of good roads and is credited with building his own custom "Brock Six."

Undaunted, William Stansell went to London to build a luxury car known as the "London Six". He produced 98 cars and delighted in driving from Windsor to Toronto, leaving Windsor 10 minutes after the train left and arriving 10 minutes before it reached Toronto.

Even that promotion didn't help his under-financed company which went bankrupt in 1925. Stansell lost everything in the venture and returned to his starting point — selling cars in Detroit.

For Many Upstarts, The Road Was Short, Rough... and Unforgiving

Although more auto companies have been launched in Windsor than any other city in Canada, competition has always been razor sharp, and unforgiving, with no room for any but the most aggressive.

For every success there was a failure. Companies started, only to disappear or be absorbed, leaving virtually no trace. In some cases the final product wasn't sound. In others, the price was too high. It took money, brains and determination to develop the production techniques necessary to gain a toe-hold, capture public interest, and bring costs into line.

In fairness, and to the credit of those who didn't make it — it wasn't for lack of trying.

Canada's First Branch Plant

One such company was the National Cycle and Auto Company Limited — Canada's first branch plant. Founded in Windsor in 1899 by a firm from Hartford, Connecticut, the Canadian division was headed by Fred. S. Evans, who was with the Canadian Typograph Company in Windsor. The company's primary business was bicycles but it also built several automobiles including the Locomobile Steamer. It was advertised as Canada's only automobile and gained quick popularity in this young country.

Unfortunately, the bicycle market slumped in 1900 so National sold that end of the business to Canadian Cycle and Motor Company (CCM). National turned out cars for two more years before that segment also fell on hard times.

• • •

Newspapers gave full support to the young automotive industry. A front page story in *The Evening Record* on January 8, 1910 prophesied:

"Walkerville will be the automotive centre of Canada in a few years. As Detroit is the centre of the auto business in the U.S., so does Walkerville bid fair to be the centre of business in Canada. Ford has long been

Soon after the automobile made its debut on city streets and country roads, it became apparent there would be a demand for repair shops to help the hapless motorist. Elie Parent's Auto Garage and Repair Works was among the early ones to open in Windsor.

successfully established with some of its machines even finding their way to far-off India...

"The Regal recently purchased seven acres near Askin's Point and erected a building. The machinery is on the ground and they will be ready to commence operations as soon as the power is installed. The E-M-F company that is to occupy the Globe premises is getting machinery, and another company, Dominion Motors Company Limited will likely locate in either Windsor or Walkerville — the automotive centre of the Dominion."

But it took more than boosterism to guarantee success:

Within a year, legal action was taken against Regal by an unpaid supplier, and Dominion faced the ire of 65 shareholders holding $70,000 worth of stock who wanted their money back.

Regal "As Good As The Wheat"

In 1910, the Regal Motor Car Company of Canada was riding a wave of optimism. It moved into Walkerville and was operated by Fred W. Haines, producing a touring car and runabout with wooden body in brown and blue.

The company produced the Regal 30, a one-ton, four-cylinder — an Eastern car with a Western slogan:

"As good as the wheat."

The phrase was meant to appeal to Prairie farmers and the car was promoted as "the car that satisfied" — but it didn't.

Salesmen drove it 5,000 miles, showing off at country fairs from Halifax to Winnipeg. The promotion never caught fire; Regal left Canada after two years and didn't return until 1951 when it opened a new plant in Kitchener.

Dominion Motors

Most Canadian auto companies were branch plants of U.S. firms or selling under license for their American counterparts. Some tried, unsuccessfully, to develop a distinctly Canadian identity.

Dominion Motors Limited of Walkerville produced the Royal Windsor Automobile, later renamed the Dominion. Despite its regal sounding name, it was a conventional car and didn't survive.

Dominion Motors was set up in January, 1910 by two Americans, A. J. Kinnucan and E. W. Winans. The plant was located at 55 Ottawa Street, just west of Monmouth Road.

The car was advertised from the Prairies to Quebec and one was even sent on a 2,000 mile trek from Walkerville to the Winnipeg Industrial Exhibition. Sales didn't follow and the company's assets were bought by Enoch Smith of Detroit. He renamed it the New Dominion Motor Car Company.

In 1915 the new firm announced it would build the Dominion truck, one of the first tractor-trailers. It was also the first Canadian company to demonstrate its truck at the Detroit Auto Show. It was a revolutionary vehicle featuring a four-wheel drive trailer and a separate two-wheel cab and engine

As early automotive engineers began to understand public tastes — and needs — they came up with ever-more attractive body designs, such as this light-duty truck used by Hiram Walker & Sons.

compartment. But it didn't find favour and the company folded that same year.

Tate Electric: 1912-1916

Tate Electric Limited of Walkerville survived from 1912 to 1916 and was the last company in Canada to produce electric passenger cars and trucks.

Tate built light delivery vans, large trucks, a roadster and a coupe. It was one of the first car makers to appeal to women in its advertising by proclaiming that it was "ideal for women after five minutes instruction..."

The car was rushed into production with unfinished models arousing interest at auto shows in Toronto and Montreal. The company boasted that the battery could be changed in about the same time as it took to fill a gas tank. The battery was long-life, light, fast-charging, powerful and was the key to the company's early success.

Production continued into 1914 but its fate was sealed with

the invention of the electric starter for gasoline-powered cars. The company was sold in 1916 to Chalmers Motor Car Company, forerunner of Chrysler Corporation.

From Tudhope To Fisher

When the Tudhope Motor Car Company went bankrupt in 1913, there were plans to develop a new plant in Windsor. Tudhope was established in Orillia, north of Toronto, in 1909. It built high-wheeled vehicles and was notable as one of the earliest, truly Canadian car makers. Its assets were bought by the Fisher Motor Car Company of Walkerville.

In 1914, Frank E. Fisher, manager of the local Studebaker plant, joined forces with F. W. Vollans of Tudhope. The plan was to sell Tudhope cars under the Fisher name, using the remaining assets of the bankrupt company. Some vehicles were assembled, while others were put together from parts.

The price was cut to $1,500 and Fisher capitalized on the Tudhope reputation, describing his cars as the result of eight years' experience in the industry. Plans to set up the factory in Walkerville collapsed, however, because the cars didn't sell.

• • •

In 1915, yet another Fisher — the Fisher Auto Body Corporation of Canada — was established on Edna Street, just east of the Pere Marquette Railway tracks. Officers of this firm were listed as F. J. Fisher, president, and C. F. Fisher, vice-president, probably referring to Fred and Charles Fisher of Detroit.

The Fisher brothers started in the U.S. in 1908. Two years later, they were awarded a major contract to build 150 car bodies for Cadillac. "Bodies by Fisher" was a well-known slogan and the company made its fortune building car bodies for Chevrolet, Chalmers, E-M-F and Studebaker, as well as Model T bodies for Ford. Shortly after McLaughlin joined GM in 1918, the Fisher plant doubled its capacity to build GM passenger car bodies. The firm finally dissolved in the late '20s. Its facilities were leased by Chrysler in 1927.

The name, Fisher Body Corporation, remained etched in stone above the front door of the Edna Street plant until the brick building burned in 1987.

LEO ST. LOUIS COLLECTION

To turn an old expression upside down, "The smaller the boys, the smaller the toys..." In this case, Frank St. Louis seems to be enjoying his 1910 Model "T" (for "Tiny") kiddycar. Sorry, there was no name plate on this advanced model.

Reo Makes Its Debut

In 1904, the Reo Motor Car Company of Canada began production in St. Catharines before establishing in Windsor in 1922. Reo was from the United States, taking its name from the initials of its founder, Ransom Eli Olds, who had already given his surname to the Oldsmobile.

Although the Reo was riding on a reputation as a big seller in the U.S., problems surfaced early. The company bought bodies from the Chatham Carriage Company, which fashioned them from pressed fibre, convinced that it would revolutionize the industry.

An early Model T chugs past Windsor City Hall.

So much for good ideas: 125 cars were built before complaints rolled in. The fibre wasn't sealed and the bodies warped or disintegrated when wet.

In 1922, Reo built the first Canadian camper trailer, a six-cylinder open car with a special rear section holding a double spring bed, tent and camping supplies.

The same year the company left St. Catharines and moved to Windsor, where it lasted another six years, assembling trucks at its plant at Church and Chatham Streets — the same building later occupied by the Packard Motor Car Company.

In 1922 Windsor police bought a Reo as a patrol car, eventually converting it to a truck. When that was junked, its parts were used in an old street sweeper. Reo dropped from the scene in 1928.

Enter The Graham-Paige

Graham-Paige Motors Canada Limited opened in July, 1931 at 172 Walker Road, later moving to 2470 Wyandotte Street East.

It too was a Canadian branch plant, but the timing couldn't have been worse. The company opened two years after the '29 market crash.

Graham-Paige was the dream of three brothers, Joseph, Robert and Ray. They started in the U.S. as glassmakers using machines invented by Joseph. They turned their attention to the auto industry, using Dodge transmissions and engines in their first trucks.

The only Graham with a Canadian serial number was the Model 56, "Prosperity Six" built in 1932. The company also built a Model 57, "Bluestreak 8". They were well-produced angular and elegant cars, but the company didn't last. Graham-Paige survived four years in Canada before closing in 1935, although Graham cars were imported from the U.S. until 1940. The Graham truck became the Dodge truck line.

Four Years For Gramm Motor Truck

In 1910, Gramm Motor Truck Company of Canada began producing heavy-duty trucks in a plant on Walker Road.

During World War One, 23 Gramm trucks were shipped overseas but they performed poorly. The company's record stops at 1914.

He Tried, And Tried Again

In the early 1900s a man named McKay arrived in Essex to build cars. He got some local backing, then rented a shop and tools from Alfred Bennett, who also invested $100 to help McKay get started. Unfortunately, by 1905, McKay was out of money and out of town, the car unfinished. Bennett completed the vehicle, which resembled a poorly-made 1904 Olds. The frame was 1 1/2-inch angle iron. Whenever a wheel dropped into a hole, the frame twisted and the engine seized.

Bennett tried a heavier frame and drove his new car from Essex to Harrow and back in one day, at speeds up to 15 miles an hour. Once was enough because the frame was still too weak to take the beating.

Dreams And Dreamers

The *Evening Record* was full of stories about automotive entrepreneurs.

Tuesday, June 10, 1902:

In the minutes of Windsor's City Council meeting there is a request by S. R. DuBrie of Penetanguishene for $25,000, or a free site, to start a $100,000 plant and hire 500 men.

"The aldermen smiled up their sleeves when reference was made to Windsor's wide streets as being well adapted to test the speed of the autos."

Council referred the request to the Industrial Committee.

• • •

Wednesday, September 20, 1905:

"Two gentlemen are in town, interested in setting up an auto factory. They are reported to be experts in the making of autos. They claim to have the designs for the best gasoline engine manufactured, similar to one being tested in France. They want to build 100 machines this year and they are looking for investors."

From the day the first cars were produced, they could do almost everything better than horse-drawn vehicles — except round the right corners or find their way home. For years, milk and bread deliverymen relied on horses to make their daily rounds.

Plans For A Touring Car

In 1910, the Walker Motor Company of Walkerville planned to build the Walker Six, a touring car and roadster. C. M. Walker was chief stockholder. His firm took over the Swift Motor Car Company of Canada Limited in Chatham. Swift had one or two cars, but it's unclear whether these were prototypes actually built in Chatham or imported from the U.S.

• • •

The Paterson Auto Company of Windsor also tried to set up in 1910. Its parent company in Flint, Michigan, wanted to assemble the "Paterson 30" in Canada.

• • •

In 1913, an announcement said the Parson's Motor Car Company of Canada was buying land for a factory in Windsor to turn out 1,200 trucks. The company said it would build a

View of Ouellette Avenue shows the Prince Edward Hotel located at Park Street. In the right foreground is the customs and immigration plaza at the exit of the Detroit-Canada Tunnel.

BAXTER / LASER PRINTS

light commercial car using a positive friction drive patented by George K. Parsons of Detroit. The company was never heard from again.

"The All-Canadian Car"

Tooling was under way in 1922 by Colonial Motors Company of Walkerville to produce a car called The Canadian. Its slogan:

"The All-Canadian car."

The Canadian was designed by former Packard man, E. G. Gunn. It had a six-cylinder engine, an aluminum radiator and this country's first independent front-end suspension.

Warren Hastings, editor of *Canadian Motorist*, test-drove a prototype and declared it impressive, allowing him to travel the worst-rutted and worn-out roads in Toronto.

The Canadian was a luxury car with a relatively high price tag of $2,600, but it never went into production.

Promises, Promises, Promises

After a flurry of promotional announcements to attract investors, followed by false starts, interest slackened probably because of the realization that it took more than a little fast-talking to succeed in such a rough-and-tumble business.

There is passing reference made to Rollin Motors Limited in Windsor. The company is listed in the City Directory for 1925 to 1926. But it may have been no more than a sales desk and telephone.

In 1929 to 1930, the Hudson Motor Car Company had a brief fling in the Walker Power Building on Walker Road. It was just an office. Later, during the early 1950s the company produced cars in a plant in Tilbury.

Part Three:
The War Years

The outbreak of World War Two opened a whole new chapter in the history of the Canadian automotive industry. Regrettably, most of it has dimmed with the passage of time, and little is fully understood by today's generations.

Windsor's contribution is without Canadian parallel when measured in numbers of military vehicles produced. Some people, steeped in military history, go so far as to say that without the total commitment of Ford, Chrysler and General Motors, the outcome of the war would have been considerably different.

One chapter dealing with this astonishing military saga can only skim the surface, but it serves as a reminder of the role played by the Big Three on the "home front".

PREVIOUS PAGE:

More than 900,000 military vehicles were produced by Canadians during World War Two – almost half by Windsor Ford workers. This 1940 scene near Plant One on Seminole shows acres of war machines ready for shipment. Photo: Ford of Canada Archives.

Business Rivals Rally To A Cause

T he ability to pull together and rally to a national cause, while boosting production levels to unprecedented heights, was demonstrated for the first time by the Big Three during World War Two.

It was a global war, waged at a terrible cost. It was a war that pulled the Western World out of a deep economic depression. It was a war that changed Canada from an adolescent nation to an industrial power... and Windsor was at the heart of it all.

Canada's industrial war effort began in earnest at secret meetings in 1936 — a full three years before war was declared. A band of military officers, businessmen and auto engineers joined with the Department of National Defence and watched as battle clouds darkened over Europe. It was clear that war was inevitable and, when it came, specialized, technically advanced military machines would be needed in vast numbers to defeat Hitler's mighty army.

They were confident that Canada could produce those weapons of war.

Within a year, Ford designers were working hand-in-glove with the government. Ford was first to budget for military research and, when war broke in 1939, the company immediately established an experimental department in Windsor Plant One. Under the guidance of Syd Swallow, a young engineer, Ford beefed up a one-ton Ford V-8 truck, giving it the muscle for heavy military service. Instead of the customary hood hinged on both sides, Ford produced a new, "alligator" hood for quick access to the engine.

Ford's president, Wallace R. Campbell, went to Ottawa to establish the War Supply Board, forerunner of the Department of Munitions and Supply.

WILLIAM GREGG COLLECTION

Light-combat Dodge trucks were produced at Chrysler's Truck Plant One.

FORD OF CANADA ARCHIVES

Campbell was a dynamic, unabashed "company man" who never missed an opportunity to push the Ford name, even in wartime. One photo celebrating the 100,000th military vehicle to roll off Ford lines shows smiling faces of company executives, with Campbell clearly in the driver's seat, hands firmly on the wheel.

Campbell loaned more technical staff to the Canadian government than any other company and committed Ford to "provide equipment that will give our fighting men striking power superior to that of the enemy".

GM's president, Sam McLaughlin, offered GM's facilities to the government and developed Canadian military vehicle designs in the late 1930s. As the war progressed, he made a more colourful — and symbolic — gesture to the nation. Always a horse lover, McLaughlin drove his horse and buggy to his Oshawa office to save gas.

Ford and GM were first to build war machines in a rapid change-over. Ford's 45-acre plant produced five types of vehicles. Civilian and military production came off the same line but the predominant colours were khaki, olive and camouflage green and brown.

GM designed a light-duty infantry truck and troop carrier with wooden body and open cab. A year later, GM developed a four-wheel drive truck with canvas top and a new, "go-anywhere" axle. While GM's affiliated plants in Windsor didn't assemble vehicles, they did produce parts, especially engines for shipment to Oshawa.

Staff officers at the front used Ford station wagons and Buick limos fitted with blackout curtains, gun clips, fire extinguishers, tools, military log books, map containers and medical kits.

Since the U.S. was not officially at war, Chrysler, as a wholly-owned American subsidiary, was not formally consulted on vehicle design, but the Canadian division helped convert U.S. vehicles to Canadian needs.

One of the first Chrysler products was "The Scout", a modified half-ton Dodge truck combining an American cab

Ford workers put the finishing touches on a field artillery tractor before shipping it overseas.

This 1942 Mercury was the last car produced by Ford for the civilian market.

and chassis with a Canadian engine. Thousands were shipped to British forces in North Africa.

For the first time in history, car companies worked as a team. On early trucks, Ford built the cab, provided sheet metal, power-trains and V-8 engines while GM handled the chassis and axles. Twenty-five hundred GM truck chassis were equipped by Chrysler as mobile workshops to repair and maintain this highly mechanized army. Many were still in use 40 years later.

As Canada was still considered a colony and, because of the misguided assumption that anything British was superior, early Canadian prototypes had to pass British inspection. Many were rejected.

The bitter irony was that mass-production techniques in Britain did not match those in North America. British truck cabs, fenders and hoods were assembled as one unit, rather than three. The system was bulky, inflexible and required a lot of hand-fitting. British designs weren't easily built on this side of the Atlantic.

Not all designs were practical. One, a tank with a small gun on a very large chassis, was conceived in a bar in Quebec's Chateau Frontenac Hotel. The story involves a senior official of Munitions and Supply and a British officer, wearing the uniform of a Royal Tank Corps captain who claimed to have experience in armoured vehicle design in North Africa.

The Canadian official, trying to make a name for himself, bypassed the Army Engineering Design Branch and sent the hasty design directly to the chief engineer at Ford in Windsor, where a prototype was built according to specs.

With the engine mounted backward, it had one forward and four reverse gears. An investigation showed that the officer was a lieutenant with no technical background. He had only been in North Africa as a prisoner escort. The whole affair was whitewashed, though it was a source of considerable amusement to the Army Engineering Design Branch.

Britain believed it could provide all of its own military

GENERAL MOTORS ARCHIVES

GM Took Pride In Its War Effort ... And Its Workers

GM was proud of its war effort on the home front and trumpeted its workers' achievements in a company publication called *War Craftsman.* In Windsor there were two GM subsidiaries, the Walkerville Engine Plant and Border Cities Industries.

The BCI gun plant earned a three-star Victory Loan flag for putting 15 per cent of its payroll into Victory Bonds in 1944.

GM sponsored billboards encouraging people to provide gifts from home for "the boys overseas". Workers donated books and blood, and collected money to send powdered milk to Britain. They also made up troop packages that included soap, razor blades, smokes and chocolates.

In 1944, BCI established an honour roll as a tribute to the 122 employees serving overseas. The company also published a special edition of *War Craftsman,* recognizing the war's casualties.

A GM War Production album was distributed to all employees, congratulating them for their work leading to victory.

needs and it wasn't until the 1940 Dunkirk fiasco, when almost 80,000 machines were left on the beaches, that the British realized they needed help in a hurry.

Since the Americans were still neutral and Australia was too distant, Canada — an international leader in automotive manufacturing — was challenged to rebuild England's arsenal. By war's end, Canada was providing machines for the entire British Empire.

Most were from Windsor.

Canada produced more than 900,000 military vehicles, almost half by Ford. GM followed with 300,000. GM also contributed aircraft frames, gun mounts and thousands of .50-calibre machine guns from a subsidiary, the Border Cities Plant in Windsor. Chrysler built 180,000 war machines. To save valuable shipping space, some vehicles manufactured here were knocked down, crated and shipped overseas, where Canadian mechanics put them back together.

In 1940, Ford designed a scout car called the Lynx, the first Canadian-built armoured vehicle. It had independent suspension, high reverse speed and pivotal steering in front or rear wheels. It was also well plated against small arms fire. Later design changes resulted in a light, fast machine suitable for reconnaissance with full armament and radio equipment. Thirty-two hundred were built in Windsor and used in 1944 in Northwestern Europe.

Also in 1940, Britain ordered 600 Universal Carriers, an amphibious, armoured open-topped vehicle with tracked wheels, similar to a tank. They were built in Britain during the previous decade but this order came to Ford in Windsor.

A few armoured cars were built in Canada during World War One, but nothing was known about bullet-proofing or armour plate. Hamilton steelmakers developed a carbon alloy material and Canada was in business. The process was adopted by American and British manufacturers. The Dominion Bridge Company made the hulls in an old plant reopened for the purpose.

Ford was the only Canadian manufacturer of Universal

Many specialized vehicles were produced in large numbers by Chrysler Canada, to meet the specific needs of the Allied forces overseas. Above is a three-ton cab-over-engine lorry. Below is a Dodge one-ton panel truck. These and many others were produced by Chrysler workers in Windsor.

Ford employees Syd Swallow (at the wheel) and Kuno Stockelbach played key roles in keeping Allied war machines moving.

Carriers, so the company gave the project top priority. Campbell assigned Jim Ronson, a young engineer, to do the job. A small assembly line was set up to build 10 prototypes. Tests were run in a special waterproof bay. In less than eight months production was transferred to a new $700,000 assembly line.

These versatile machines were known as "Battle Taxis" because they carried troops, flame throwers and other gun mounts. The flame throwers, dubbed "Ronson Lighters", had a range of up to 90 yards.

Many UCs were used in Canada for airfield defences on the northwest coast of B.C. Others were shipped to Europe and North Africa, where the engines were rebuilt every 2,000 to 3,000 miles because of the punishing desert heat and sand.

Success of the UCs in North Africa led to more British orders in 1943. The ultimate was the Windsor carrier "Mark One". Used as an anti-tank weapon, it was longer and heavier and could tow a gun across difficult terrain under small arms fire.

On August 17, 1944, Ford celebrated 40 years in production, featuring the 27,678th Universal Carrier built. By the end of the year, when the Windsor carrier was taken off the secret list, the new machine was showcased in Ford advertisements.

"Rosie The Rivetter" Had A Windsor Counterpart

Much has been made of the role of women working in industry, replacing men on active military service. Up to half the workers in some ammunition and auto parts plants were women.

In Windsor, they worked at Gotfredson Truck and Border Cities Industries. They trained at W. D. Lowe Secondary School, wore coveralls, tied their hair back and worked as rivetters, lathe operators and inspectors.

In the U.S., "Rosie the Rivetter" was prominent in wartime propaganda, but in Windsor it was "Ruthie the Rivetter". She was 16-year-old Ruth Dunn, who worked at Border Cities Industries.

While women were given tax incentives and provided with day-care assistance, it was still a man's world in the plants.

Women were less prevalent in vehicle assembly plants because of heavy lifting requirements. Instead, they were usually relegated to shipping and receiving departments. Ford's wartime promotional films show few female workers, and after 1942 they were excluded from the plants altogether.

Ford sponsored the Women's Auxiliary Motor Service, training women to drive tractors and trucks and to change tires. More than 12,000 women enrolled across Canada.

Ford trucks lined up for final inspection before being shipped overseas.

Civilian car production was reduced in 1941 and halted in 1942 as the war intensified. While the government encouraged greater war production it set aside 4,500 cars nationwide for doctors, nurses, police and firefighters.

Stan Ellis, manager of Ford's service department in Windsor, was sent to England to supervise a vehicle assembly plant. Foremen were also supplied by Ford and GM in Canada. They worked out of the Canadian Mechanization Depot in Southampton, England, until the plant was destroyed by enemy bombers. By war's end, 100,000 units were assembled in England.

There were 32 other assembly locations in Britain, North Africa, Italy and Australia. Canada supplied one third of all the vehicles used by the British forces in the Middle East and half of the transport vehicles used by Montgomery's Desert Rats to defeat Rommel's Afrika Korp.

Ford personnel from Windsor staffed all British 8th Army repair depots. One of those assigned to North Africa was Kuno Stockelbach who spent three years in Ford's Windsor service department starting in 1930. Stockelbach, a no-nonsense South African, directed the assembly of 150 vehicles a day despite pilfering by Bedouin tribesmen, who wrapped spark plugs in leather thongs and wore them as ornaments.

By 1942, Ford had undergone several expansions. The company had four assembly lines compared to one before the war, and employed 15,000 people. It had already built 130,000 military vehicles including water tankers, vans and trucks; anti-aircraft tractors as well as a three-ton derrick, gun and personnel carriers, dump trucks, station wagons, buses, ambulances and lorries.

Above, Ford President Wallace Campbell and a staff officer with the Department of National Defence stand symbolically on guard in one of Ford's go-anywhere Universal Carriers. Below, Number 28,988, the last UC produced, left the Ford plant in January 1945.

The company even designed CBC field recording units.

Ford's four-wheel drive trucks, nicknamed "Blitz Buggies" and "Benghazi Fords" were designed by the Canadian Traction Company of Windsor. Gotfredson Truck of Walkerville built 23,000 field artillery bodies for Ford and GM.

Meanwhile, GM's 13,500 workers were busy building armoured combat and reconnaissance cars, ambulances, cable layers, mobile and field offices, dental clinics, lorries, dump and general trucks, as well as water and gas tankers.

GM subsidiaries also built airplane fuselages, naval guns, armoured vehicles and anti-tank gun carriages. Ford and GM built three-ton lorries. Some were equipped as mobile kitchens, others served as office and living quarters for field officers.

Chrysler had 3,400 employees in Windsor, Regina and Chatham producing gun ports, ammunition sights, special motors, bridging equipment, combat units and refuelling tenders. Chrysler parts plants shipped millions of pounds of rocket tubes and shells.

On June 19, 1943, Canadian production reached half a million units. The occasion was marked by presentation of a three-ton, four-by-four, Windsor-built Ford to the federal government. The celebration in Oshawa drew presidents and technicians from the Big Three. The truck also had the logos of all three companies on its grille. Representatives of 200 other allied industries involved in war production attended.

Because of this tremendous war effort, the Canadian army was the most highly mechanized in the world, boasting one vehicle for every three soldiers in Europe.

Even the enemy acknowledged the superiority of Canadian vehicles. Propaganda films of the day suggest there was a standing order by German high command not to destroy Canadian vehicles, as they were superior to German-made models.

Notwithstanding these Olympian achievements, little attention has been paid to this important chapter in Canada's manufacturing saga — or to the role Windsor played in developing superior military machines.

Part Four:
The Changing Times

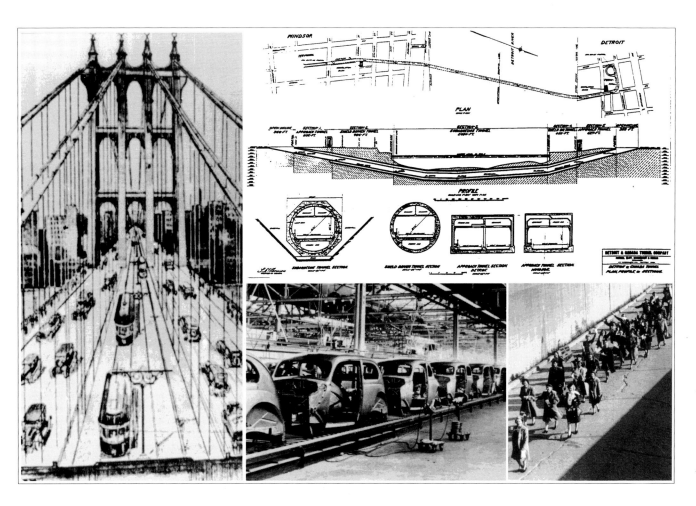

Henry Ford and Gordon McGregor were audacious visionaries; men who could dream, yet not make dreams their master. When they joined forces in 1904 it's likely that challenges of the moment left little time to muse about the impact they would make on the future.

Great highways, bridges and tunnels were built. No longer confined to crowded cities, people could move to newly-created suburbs. Quality-of-life was no longer left to the vagaries of chance.

There were new jobs, better wages — and challenges for workers to unite for common causes. New laws and international agreements were framed, responding to the changing times. As none of these could have been foreseen in 1904, neither can we imagine what future generations will face as the industry grows and matures.

PREVIOUS PAGE:

Could anyone have possibly imagined the social and economic upheaval that lay in store as we entered the 20th Century — the Age of the Automobile? Not likely — but nothing had such a profound effect on the nation as the coming of the car.

Far left:
When plans were being laid for construction of the Ambassador Bridge, one of the concepts offered was a span open, not only to automotive and pedestrian traffic, but trains and street cars as well.
Illustration: François Baby House Museum.

Top right:
One of the much-talked-about marvels of contemporary engineering was the Detroit-Canada Tunnel.
Graphic: Detroit-Canada Tunnel Corporation.

Bottom centre:
Once the concept of assembly-line production was accepted, improvements came rapidly as car companies sought faster and cheaper ways of getting their products to market.
Photo: Windsor Star library.

Bottom right:
Before the 1945 UAW strike of the Ford Motor Company had run its course, almost everyone in Windsor got into the act... including wives, mothers and daughters of striking workers. They marched in public protest and took refreshments to those on picket duty.
Photo: Windsor Star library.

Bridge And Tunnel End The Steam Ferry Era

F or many years the only commercial link between Windsor and Detroit was provided by steam-powered ferries. In their heyday, as many as 20 or 30 plied the Detroit River, Lakes St. Clair and Erie at any given time.

Some were small passenger boats, others were large enough to carry horse-drawn wagons or freight train boxcars.

The highly competitive service among shipping companies picked up in the early 20th Century with the arrival of automobiles on both sides of the river.

By the 1920s, it became clear that the ferries could not keep up with the rapidly increasing motorized traffic. Waiting lines grew longer with every passing week and the need for better, faster, more efficient systems was critical.

Incredibly, two different solutions came into existence within a year of each other. The Ambassador Bridge, carrying vehicles over the water, opened on November 11, 1929, and the underwater tunnel opened on November 3, 1930. Both were remarkable engineering achievements for the time, and made a tremendous impact on the social and commercial ties of two communities in two different countries.

Although many motorists favoured the bridge or tunnel, ferry boat companies refused to concede defeat and launched a fare-price war in their fight for survival. Finally, the Detroit & Windsor Ferry Company marked the end of an era, serving notice that it would no longer continue after July 18, 1938.

CARL MORGAN COLLECTION

The Cadillac was one of the many steam ferries forced out of business after the bridge and tunnel were opened. Launched in 1928 to carry cars and passengers between Windsor and Detroit, it was the largest and most powerful steamer on North American waters.

1834.

S TEAM BOAT FERRY.—The STEAM BOAT ARGO, having been fitted up and put in complete repair, will hereafter be employed as a FERRY BOAT between the City of Detroit and the Beacon Ferry House, Sandwich. The proprietor has been at considerable pains and expense in rendering the Argo an expeditious and commodiou medium of communication between the above mentioned places; and the public may rely on being accommodated without delay or inconvenience in the conveyance of Carriages and Waggons of all kinds, Cattle, Horses, &c. &c.

The above arrangement is intended by the proprietor to be permanent; and for the necessary and frequent communication between the Canada side and Detroit, be hopes the public will extend to him patronage sufficient to compensate him for his enterprise. The proprietor will bestow his whole attention to this business, and will spare no exertions in rendering the Steam Ferry a highly convenient and safe mode of conveyance.

The construction of the boat is such that no inconvenience will be experienced by gentlemen and ladies who may cross with teams or horses, as there is a spacious deck, gentlemen and ladies' cabin, where passengers may retire with safety and comfort.

L. DAVENPORT.

Sept. 10, 1832.

Perhaps because of its proximity to the automotive district, which was concentrated between Walker Road and Drouillard Road, the Walkerville Ferry dock (above) was a busy customs point of entry.

Thousands of cars stream over the Ambassador Bridge and through the Detroit-Canada Tunnel. It was the convenience and swift movement of cars that sounded the death knell for the proud steam ferries that plied the Detroit River for decades.

FRANÇOIS BABY HOUSE MUSEUM

CARL MORGAN COLLECTION

A mucker uses a power knife to slice away the clay during construction of the Detroit-Canada Tunnel.

Bus companies and car owners lost no time in making full use of the tunnel. It provided a quick and direct link between the commercial hearts of Detroit and Windsor.

FRANÇOIS BABY HOUSE MUSEUM

Traffic control lights, in the centre of main intersections, like this one in Kingsville, were soon part of the Canadian scene.

Petroleum companies under-stood the value of high-profile advertising, and eye-catching signs sprouted across the land.

Tariffs: Rx For Industrial Health

As trade barriers come down and the world moves toward a global economy, it's useful to know that in the early 1900s the tariff walls were necessary to protect struggling Canadian manufacturers.

It was a question of economies of scale. Canadian goods were pricier than American because Canada's market was small and spread over thousands of miles. Manufacturers were not able to produce enough volume to lower costs.

Tariffs are designed to raise import prices to the same level as domestic goods. For instance, the duty on carriages entering Canada was 35 per cent. The Americans wanted a slice of our market, but didn't want to pay the price.

For a few years, there was a brisk trade in luxury cars smuggled across the border by dealers who saved one third of the cost. Alarmed Canadian car builders demanded that the government toughen border restrictions.

Always resourceful, the Americans found a solution. The duty on parts was lower than on a fully assembled car, so they shipped their parts for assembly. The finished product, made in Canada, was sold at a reduced rate of duty.

In some cases, American companies let Canadians develop and run the factories on Canadian soil. In others, the Americans set up their own plants. Either way, these "branch plants" impeded the growth of Canadian-born manufacturers. Canadian companies were either swallowed up or driven under by American giants.

Although not all Canadians were satisfied with the practice, both sides benefitted. Canadians gained jobs, while the Americans gained access to both the Canadian and British markets. As a colony, Canada enjoyed reciprocal trade with Britain. It was cheaper to ship goods from Canada to Australia, New Zealand, South Africa, Siam and Morocco. The entire British Empire opened up to the American auto industry.

By 1920 there were 252,000 cars and 22,000 commercial vehicles on Canadian roads. Canada's auto industry ranked sixth in terms of Gross National Product, the fourth major auto manufacturer in the world, with half the cars exported.

Nine years later Canada was the second largest car maker behind the U.S., producing 203,000 passenger cars and 59,000 trucks. Sixty-four thousand cars were exported and half of the trucks were shipped overseas. Those production levels were not repeated for 20 years.

Times were good and the industry grew until the Depression. During five devastating years, Canadian manufacturers lost as much as $100 a car at the worst, or earned 75 cents at best. To balance the scales, Prime Minister R. B. Bennett again raised tariffs to prevent wholesale "dumping" in Canada.

The success of the industry depended largely on the tariff. Rates fluctuated wildly on the whims of government.

Ironically, tariffs annoyed Canadians — the people they were supposed to protect. Canadians wanted lower American prices — and gave little thought of what that meant to their jobs or survival of industry in this country.

Canadians were paying $265 more than Americans for the same car. Conditions were so bad that a Board of Inquiry investigated whether tariffs were costing Canadians too much by keeping car prices artificially high.

W. R. Campbell, president of Ford of Canada, felt the government had to support the auto industry because manufacturers put so much money into it. He argued that companies not only built cars but helped develop towns, cities, railways and natural resources.

The battle divided the nation and, in 1936, the tariff on imports was replaced by a constant duty of 17.5 per cent on imported cars. The duty remained for 30 years.

Despite these tariff wars — or perhaps because of them — the Big Three dominated car production by 1933. Studebaker manufacturer Walter Flanders accurately prophesied:

"The history of this industry will be the story of a conflict between giants."

Or, as one Canadian nationalist suggested, "the Canadian auto industry settled down to become a pale copy of the United States."

BAXTER / LASER PRINTS

It wasn't long after the automobile grabbed the public imagination that gasoline pumps popped up like tulips in spring.

Learning how to build a car that ran reasonably well was one thing; learning how to build them on a mass production basis to cut costs and make them more affordable was the trick. It didn't happen overnight, but car makers worked out the wrinkles, one by one.

Above: Magneto flywheels move along between guide rails as each worker performs his particular part of the assembly operation.

Right: A rubber tire is fitted to a wooden rim.

A Touch Of Wizardry Made The Difference

There's a great deal of mechanical wizardry in the way that cars are built today, compared with 80 or 90 years ago. The differences are so vast as to be almost incomprehensible.

Life in today's auto plant is quieter, cleaner, less frantic. Since the line is mechanized and robotized there is little heavy lifting and, in some areas, there is an unsettling absence of humans.

Mammoth presses stamp out fenders, dashboards and gas tanks; sheet metal is shaped in one press then automatically transferred to another. Shock absorbers, springs, axles, brakes, steering, transmission, engine, rear axle, radiator, muffler, bumpers, tires and wheels are added to the frame, followed by doors, windows, and trim.

It's a remarkable process involving more than 15,000 parts pieced together in 1,800 operations. In one Windsor plant, for example, 1,100 cars are completed each day, six days a week. An engine is installed every 50 seconds.

Ninety years ago, factories were small, noisy and dirty. They were cold in winter and stifling hot in summer. A few dozen workers finished two or three cars a week. Prolonged cold spells closed plants until a system was developed to blow heat through a tube, warming the wooden floors.

Usually the buildings were long and narrow. Rough stock entered one end and moved through as many as 20 departments, before emerging as a complete car. Metal parts went to the machine shop to be hammered, shaped, drilled and welded before being attached to car bodies which were then moved to the paint, varnish, upholstery and testing divisions.

Chassis straddled stationary wooden trestles as workers selected parts from stockpiles and carried them to the car. In larger plants, long rows of frames sat side-by-side on the floor, waiting the arrival of workmen carrying tools and adding parts from nearby stockpiles.

The process worked in a fashion, but it was costly and

inefficient. Men were in each other's way causing bottlenecks. Metals were brittle and the machining was far from precise.

Henry Ford was the first to adopt mass production methods, setting the pace for the rest of the industry. He needed a system that ran smoothly, cut costs and increased production. He found it, of all places, in the Chicago meat packing industry where carcasses swung along on overhead trolleys.

Ford simply substituted car parts for beef sides and was on his way to developing the first moving assembly line in the auto industry. He installed iron slides on two railway ties, mounted a chassis on top and pulled the whole contraption around the plant. Parts were bolted or welded at each stop.

Before the assembly line, workers carried parts to the car but, by 1910, the car moved to the parts. Once the wheels were attached, the vehicle was pushed from station-to-station as men hammered, cut, milled and drilled gear cases, fuel tanks, headlamps and other parts. At the Ford plant, radiators were assembled on a second floor. The bodies were fitted into place from above, using gravity to lower them into place. The new system cut labour, cost and time.

By 1912, Ford used a combination of overhead trolleys, conveyors, slides and rollways to move parts to work areas where men assembled sub-units including axles, frames, motors and dashboards. As each new Ford was finished and gassed, a tester jumped into the driver's seat, slipped the car into gear and let it roll down a steep runway, cranking itself into life.

This was the first time material handling systems were used in car manufacturing, but the continuously moving assembly line was still to come. To achieve that, parts had to be standardized, machined to close tolerances, handled efficiently and installed at precisely the right moment as the line moved.

Until 1913, a skilled worker could assemble a flywheel magneto in 20 minutes. When the job was split into 29 operations on a moving line, time was cut to 13 minutes.

In 1914, the moving line was raised to a more comfortable

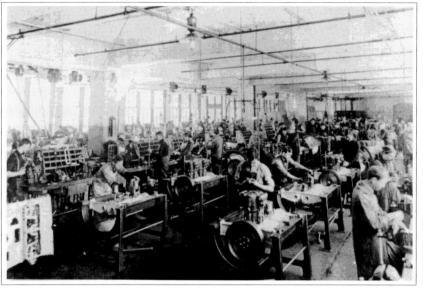

Above: Skilled workmen assemble engines held solidly in special, stationary cradles.

Left: Quality control depends largely on the skills of workers like this drill press operator.

Final inspection and last-minute touches are made before finished cars move out of the plant and into dealerships.

As frames for 1925 Model T Fords move along the assembly line, they are mated with bodies lowered from an overhead conveyor system.

working level. A time-and-motion study showed the line speed could increase and one man could do the work of four. Within a year Ford reduced assembly time from 12 hours, to six. Two hundred and fifty assemblers and 80 parts carriers took almost a month to complete 6,000 chassis in 1913. The next year, those production figures doubled!

Although every change brought savings, the key to success was the development of a continuous chain with lugs that caught each chassis and pulled it along at a pre-set speed past workers who installed parts from other moving lines. With such improvements, assembly time was cut to 2 1/2 hours. Crew sizes increased and production time dropped by another hour.

Not surprisingly, there was a price to pay in morale. Workers were unhappy, but they grumbled quietly for fear of losing their jobs.

Henry Ford had a reputation of being good to his workers. In Detroit in 1914, he introduced the eight-hour day, and boosted wages to $5 from $2.50 a day — an astonishing sum for the times.

The next year, Gordon McGregor announced that Windsor workers would get $4 a day and the work week was reduced to 48 hours.

Newspapers reported there was a momentary hush, then pandemonium, as workers cheered, shouted and threw their hats and caps into the air. They wore company badges as a sign of their loyalty. They belonged to the industrial elite, making two dollars a day more while working two hours less than workers elsewhere.

Businessmen questioned the soundness of the increase. It cost $600,000, but Ford reasoned that higher wages meant better workers and increased production.

The philosophy worked — and so did the men. The pace was gruelling but, because of the intense output, year-round employment was not guaranteed. At times workers endured long, tough, payless layoffs.

Still, the system worked for Ford. There was a labour shortage in the U.S. and half the workforce drifted in and out of factories, finding other jobs as the spirit took them. Ford's well-paid hands stayed longer, eliminating the need to train newcomers.

Besides, people with money bought cars.

The move brought the automobile out of the luxury class and made it afforable to the common man.

Delegates were in a celebratory mood as they attended the first Collective Bargaining Convention of the infant Canadian Auto Workers Union in 1987. The occasion marked the end of a long, exhausting battle for independence by Canadian auto workers, who felt that contracts negotiated in the U.S. were no longer acceptable to Canadian workers.

Canadian Auto Workers Fought Long And Hard For Full Autonomy

To write about the auto industry without mentioning unions, is to write about boats, without mentioning water.

Organized labour arrived in Windsor in August, 1902, with the birth of the Border Cities Trade and Labour Council. By 1918, there were 33 locals with 3,700 members, chiefly skilled tradesmen. The first auto workers' union in Canada was the United Automobile Aircraft and Vehicle Workers of America which started in 1920 but didn't last the year. It was followed by the American Federation of Labour (AFL).

In 1935, the United Auto Workers-Congress of Industrial Organizations was formed at a convention in Indiana — and Canadian auto workers were on common ground.

Windsor's first UAW local was Kelsey Motor Wheel Com-pany. Its 100 members became Local 195 on December 11, 1936. Within five days the workers joined GM employees in Oshawa and St. Catharines in a sitdown strike — the newest labour weapon.

Union activists felt that such actions were necessary to gain recognition, though they did divide public opinion. Ontario Premier Mitch Hepburn was anti-union and vowed the CIO would not get into Ontario. Conversely, one-time Windsor mayor, David Croll, then provincial labour minister said he would rather march with the workers than with GM — and marched out of cabinet.

Union organization wasn't for the faint-hearted, especially in the U.S. where violence was common. The most infamous

In 1979, Doug Fraser (left) then president of the UAW, led negotiations with Chrysler Corporation, while Bob White, president of the Canadian Region, wrestled with GM and Ford in an effort to achieve a contract tailored for Canadian needs.

incident was the 1937 Battle of the Overpass at the Ford plant on the Rouge River, when company goons beat up unionists who were distributing leaflets. Despite the attack, strikers held out stubbornly for four years before the company yielded.

The UAW was certified at Ford of Canada on December 1, 1941, and Windsor Ford Local 200 received its charter, making it the oldest Ford union in Canada. After a brief strike in 1942, the union won equal pay for equal work but Ford countered by refusing to hire women. Continued labour disputes led to walkouts and work interruptions during the war.

In the early 1950s, the UAW gained its first company-paid pension plan with the slogan *"Too old to work, too young to die".* The auto workers also negotiated Boxing Day followed by a Christmas-New Year shutdown.

UAW president Walter Reuther earned a reputation as a powerful orator with a rivetting personality and a deep concern for the welfare of his members. He impressed Bob White, a young Canadian shop steward, when he said that unions had to be active in national and world affairs as well as plant issues.

White was a street-smart Irishman who came to Canada in 1949 and worked in a Stratford woodworking factory. He spent half his time on union business, working up the ladder after falling into the job by default.

Not all Canadians were sold on unions, particularly those with close ties to the big American organizations. Some felt unions were Communist-dominated and that membership drives were intended only to fatten union coffers. They also believed that, if the UAW struck a plant, everyone had to strike and they would lose their jobs.

White had a tough job changing that thinking but, by the 1950s, 30,000 workers were organized and wages were among the highest in Canada. They won a guaranteed annual wage and Supplementary Unemployment Benefits, providing them with 95 per cent of their pay during a lay-off.

Other UAW firsts include:
• Prescription drug plan.
• Survivor pension benefits paid by the company.
• Cost of Living Allowance (COLA).
• Family health care programs.
• Wage parity for auto workers.

White's star was rising. In 1960, at 25, he was the youngest union employee. During those years he listened to leaders who talked about special status for Canada. One of them was Dennis McDermott who replaced George Burt in 1968 as director of the Canadian Region.

A year later, McDermott, brash, outspoken and volatile, moved the Canadian headquarters from Windsor to Toronto. While that angered Windsor unionists, McDermott felt it was time the Canadian union fled the shadow of the American eagle. The die was cast.

In 1970, McDermott won special status for the Canadian Region. He became an international UAW vice-president, ensuring Canadians a voice in the American union. Articulate, provocative, media-wise, McDermott was good for the union profile and politicians paid attention.

During a GM strike in 1970, American workers settled first, leaving Canadians on the line and making a mockery of the strike slogan, *"Out Together, In Together"*. The international rift widened.

A similar situation occurred in 1973 during talks with Chrysler. The big issue concerned voluntary overtime. Workers wanted to prevent the company from forcing them to work extra hours. In Windsor, Chrysler Local 444 already had a gentleman's agreement that overtime was voluntary after 48 hours. It was a hard-fought battle that the local won by filing a blizzard of grievances. Windsor workers hoped to include it in the new contract.

Most of the bargaining was done in Detroit, without input from Windsor. Eventually, the UAW accepted voluntary overtime after 56 hours, which meant Windsor workers actually lost ground.

During Ford talks that year, the company assumed that Canadians would follow the unwritten rule and sign the American agreement. This time, McDermott made it clear that Canada was not the U.S. and the Canadian region wouldn't swallow what he called "American bilge."

The Canadians hung tough and won a better contract than their U.S. counterparts. The message was out: Canadians would no longer rubber stamp American settlements.

McDermott continued his quest for independence. He'd already started publishing his all-Canadian *"Solidarity"* newspaper, rather than accept space in the American publication. When the Canadian Region at the UAW International Conference was lumped in with the American delegation under the Stars and Stripes, McDermott complained. The Canadians fought for, and won, independent affiliation.

For the first time, the Canadian flag made an appearance at

CAW / WINDSOR

George Burt:
Long Service Tribute
from Local 240 in 1982

Dennis McDermott:
Moved UAW Headquarters
to Toronto in 1969

international union meetings.

In 1978, McDermott left the UAW to head the Canadian Labour Congress and White took over, picking Bazil "Buzz" Hargrove, a young lieutenant, as his assistant.

North America was heading into a major recession, rocking the auto industry and the union. Over 15,000 workers were laid off, plants closed and car companies suffered huge losses.

Suddenly, unions had to deal with new problems such as the advance of robotics, keeping work in Canada, and the low Canadian dollar. It was apparent that Canadian negotiators had different priorities, dealing with different labour laws and a radically different health care system. Agreements settled in the U.S. just didn't fit in Canada. White argued that Canada was "not a region, but a country."

A proud, new, Canadian logo

During the 1979 negotiations, Ford and GM bargained separately in Canada but Windsor Chrysler workers weren't ready to cut the umbilical cord. UAW head, Doug Fraser, a veteran of the Chrysler assembly line and trusted by Canadian workers, led the negotiations while White tussled with GM and Ford.

Chrysler convinced the workers to delay their contract settlement by six months, giving the company time to get back on its feet. Fraser agreed, even though it cost Canadian and U.S. workers $203,000,000.

Conditions deteriorated for Chrysler. When big cars stopped selling, the automaker cut the work force at its Windsor engine plant from 2,200 to 450. The company went back to the workers, saying it needed $8 billion to compete. Cuts were negotiated to show that the union was serious about helping the company survive.

Canadian members with Local 444 were powerless to influence the talks and were so infuriated they were ready to strike. They wanted to hang Fraser, White and Iacocca in effigy until union leaders Ken Gerard and Larry Bauer calmed them down.

When Chrysler asked for government loan guarantees in the U.S., the government asked that the UAW contract be renegotiated. The Canadians refused. In December, 1980, Iacocca met with Fraser and agreed to a freeze on wages and pensions, fewer paid holidays and the elimination of COLA, (Cost of Living Allowance). Iacocca called it a super deal while the union labelled it the worst economic settlement ever.

In Canada, the union made no recommendations and the agreement was accepted by only 51 percent. From then on, Canadian negotiators refused to accept concessions, despite pressure from the Big Three. Even Ken Gerard, a staunch supporter of the UAW, agreed that it was time to break away.

As Chrysler fought for survival, a bail-out package was worked out on both sides of the border. To make it happen, the Canadian government guaranteed a $200,000,000 bank loan. Chrysler was living week-to-week and time was running out.

Windsor's tireless Herb Gray, then Federal Minister of Industry, carried the ball and Ottawa finally bought into the deal after Chrysler agreed to produce a new wagon and front-wheel-drive car in Windsor.

Meantime, Chrysler workers left the international nest and negotiated their own contract for the first time. Talks moved to Toronto for better media coverage and to escape the Detroit influence.

The union allowed five weeks before the strike deadline — but Windsor was impatient. Tempers flared and some workers walked out. The company threatened disciplinary action which triggered a wildcat. They set bonfires, tipped a truck, and chased union officials. The scene grew ugly, forcing White to send Gerard and Hargrove to get the men back to work.

Talks collapsed, and workers struck on November 5.

In a show of solidarity, Canadian and American workers agreed not to settle one contract without the other. Some Americans joined Windsor's picket line. When agreement was reached, Canadian workers pocketed 50 cents more than their American counterparts.

During the 1982 talks, GM workers made labour history when they negotiated an agreement paying them more than workers in the U.S. McDermott toasted the deal with champagne saying:

"Today GM recognized that Canada is a foreign country."

In the 1984 talks with GM, similar differences involving Canadian autonomy surfaced and the UAW rift became a chasm. UAW president Owen Bieber wanted to know whether they were one union or two? He rejected White's argument that they were one union with different priorities. He threatened to revoke Canada's strike authorization.

Canadians ignored the warning and struck, putting 40,000 American workers on lay-off. When the 12-day strike ended 80 per cent of Canadian workers voted for a contract different from the U.S. The agreement included child care, pre-paid legal services and affirmative action for women. White called it a breakthrough and openly challenged the UAW for more Canadian autonomy.

After much agonizing the way cleared for separation but Americans were still reluctant, fearing that if the Canadians left, it would shred the union.

The pain of separation wasn't over. Canadians wanted $60,000,000 as their share of UAW assets. They were offered $20,000,000 and settled on $36,000,000.

The founding convention of the Canadian branch was held in Toronto in 1985 — the 50th anniversary of the UAW. Bieber refused to attend, nor would he part with the $36,000,000 — or allow the Canadians to use the UAW name. He said it was "copyrighted."

The situation frustrated Canadian staff member Sam Gindin, director of research and later assistant to the president. As Bob White recalled in his book *Hard Bargains*, Gindin suggested the new union be called the Canadian Brewery and Salt Workers, or the CBASW. He said that, when you take out the "B.S.", you end up with the same initials anyway.

The UAW sent a congratulatory message tinged with bitterness — but it acknowledged Canada's right to separate. It wasn't until 1993 that Bieber took steps to end the rift.

The convention was a high point for White. The new union

Although adversaries at the bargaining table, M. J. (Moe) Closs, president of Chrysler (left), and Ken Gerard, president of Local 444, often put their differences aside to work for a common cause — in this case, the 1989 United Way campaign.

didn't have any money or a name — but it was all-Canadian. More than 1,000 delegates from 115 locals listened proudly as Victor Reuther, brother of Walter — the old war horse who led the UAW in 1946 — supported the Canadian break. He recognized Canada's nationalistic feelings and told the delegates they didn't need unity with the U.S. to have solidarity.

The Canadian Auto Workers united 140,000 Canadian workers — 100,000 directly involved in the auto industry. It represented Canada's largest manufacturing sector on which the Canadian economy depended.

The CAW became the sixth largest union in Canada. When Hargrove replaced White as president in 1992, he represented a new look for the union. Fifty thousand members worked for the Big Three and, with auto parts plant workers, still over half of the CAW members worked in the industry.

week until the company requires more production than can be reasonably anticipated to result from operations at forty hours per week.

GENERAL

60. When an employee is transferred to a higher paid classification he will within one hundred and sixty hours of work in that classification be paid the rate of such classification.

61. As far as reasonably possible overtime and extra time will be equitably distributed among those employees on the same shift normally performing the relevant work to be done.

62. The union will not cause or permit its members to cause, nor will any member of the union take part in any sit-down, stay-in or slow-down in any plant of the company, or any curtailment of work or restriction of or interference with production of the company. The union will not cause or permit its members to cause, nor will any member of the union take part in any strike or stoppage of any of the plants or premises of the company until all of the grievance procedure outlined herein shall have been exhausted and not even then unless authorized by International Executive Board of the U.A.W.-C. ization shall have been ...

Subject to the pro tions, in the event a be terminated by such termination to

The company r employee who vio

In the event of who are exclud agreement, the ployees in the the company

ing unit who may violate this section by engaging in any strike, picketing, sit-down, stay-in, slow-down or any other curtailment of work or restriction or interference with production of the company.

The company will not cause or sanction a lock-out until all of the grievance procedure outlined herein shall have been exhausted.

Subject to the provisions of government regulations, in the event such a lock-out occurs this agreement may be terminated by the union upon notification of such termination to the company by the union.

In the event of the occurrence of a dispute between the company and employees the union agrees that it will at all times during the currency of this agreement take such steps as may be necessary to ensure that employees employed in the Power House or any sub-station of the company shall be permitted free and unobstructed entrance into and exit from the premises and plants of the company in order that such employees may at all times be enabled to perform the regular duties therein to which they are assigned.

In the event of the occurrence of a dispute between the company and employees the union agrees that it will co-operate with the company to ensure that employees required for emergent maintenance repairs to the company's plants will be permitted free and unstructed entrance into and exit from such plants at that the company's plant protection staff and off that and personnel shall be allowed free and un staff and entrance into and exit from the comp ... office. Provided that if at any time ... company attempts to put an ... company's plants on ... ees in the b ... ch wo ... or atte ... repair ... union ... his par

AGREEMENT

Between

FORD MOTOR COMPANY OF CANADA, Limited

and

INTERNATIONAL UNION U.A.W.-C.I.O.

Signed February 15th, 1946

*THIS AGREEMENT COVERS ALL HOURLY-RATED EMPLOYEES IN THE BARGAINING UNIT IN THE COMPANY'S WINDSOR, ONTARIO PLANTS.

After a strike that lasted more than three months, the UAW-CIA and Ford finally came to terms. The contract was signed February 15, 1946.

BAXTER / LASER PRINTS

99 Days That Changed Everything

On September 12, 1945, with World War Two ended, Ford of Canada entered the first and toughest strike in its history — a bitter battle that took its toll on both sides and forever changed the relationship between union and management.

Weary negotiators were at an impasse after 18 months of futile talks. Many concerns were still unresolved — including the toughest — job security.

The UAW wanted seniority for returning veterans. Jobs were readily available during the war, but scarce after. The UAW also wanted a union shop with compulsory dues and membership, fearing that, without such protection, the company could destroy the movement.

As the strike erupted, police clashed with pickets during the 99-day standoff. On the first day, Ford of Canada president Wallace Campbell confronted hundreds of angry strikers who stood their ground waving placards and shouting threats when he tried to cross the line.

Roy England, Local 200 president, climbed a truck shouting: "This city will not return to the bread lines and soup kitchens of pre-war years."

Police were in a squeeze:

Attorney General Leslie Blackwell said workers had the right to picket and no action would interfere with those rights, but people with lawful business in the plant also had the right to come and go. Police stayed neutral and wouldn't offer protection to those forcing their way through. At the same time they told union officials that charges would be laid against law breakers.

On September 18, charges were laid against members of Local 200 and the air was electric with tension. Within six weeks, another major confrontation developed.

Five Ford security guards continued working at the factory, but company officials said they needed a staff of 125 to maintain its $6,000,000 power plant and provide adequate fire protection. Ford also said that untended gasoline tanks could rupture and explode. The workers wouldn't budge.

RCMP officers tend their horses after being called in to assist local and provincial police to maintain control at tension-filled picket sites around the Ford plant.

Planes, trains and cars brought in 250 RCMP and OPP officers from Montreal and Ottawa. Reports said the government might send in 300 troops. Police made their first move early in November. It ended in a shoving match, but the picket line held.

The pendulum of public opinion swung in favour of the strikers and Windsor Mayor Art Reaume vowed that "no imported police force " would break the strike.

It became a cause celebre and workers at 25 plants added muscle by marching in their off hours. Morale climbed as the numbers swelled to 8,500 including workers from GM, Chrysler, Gotfredson, Kelsey Wheel, Bendix and Dominion Forge.

Fifteen hundred Ford workers and supporters march through downtown Windsor in a mammoth show of solidarity.

In 1946, the UAW presented this honorary membership certificate to Windsor Mayor Arthur J. Reaume in recognition of his support for the union during the strike against Ford.

Other unions across the country sent telegrams, letters and money. Some took sympathy strike action of their own. Spirits were bolstered again by American Ford workers who crossed the border with a brass band, trumpets and loud speakers blaring.

The crunch came on November 5, when hundreds of cars were commandeered and jammed bumper-to-bumper, curb-to-curb around the plant. Twenty streets were gridlocked and a union boat patrolled the Detroit River to prevent access from the water.

Traffic froze for two days as more aid poured in to the determined workers living on meagre strike pay. A street dance was held each day and coffee and doughnuts were served.

The strike was heavily covered by *The Windsor Daily Star.* Editorial writers fumed that no matter who was at fault, the walkout was not justified so soon after a war when the company was still involved in military production.

Businessmen were concerned that the strike would cost them sales as other auto plants, parts and supply companies shut down. The Gotfredson Truck Company closed, laying off 500.

Tensions spread to the political arena and City Council, fearing that police action would lead to bloodshed or a general strike, called for government intervention.

Siding with the union, David Croll, Liberal member for Toronto-Spadina and former mayor of Windsor raised the question:

"Is it good for Canada to have an industry built on tariffs, an industry in which profits have been swollen, an industry which has a virtual monopoly in the manufacture of an essential commodity, refuse the workers the right to collective bargaining?"

After more than two months, the union allowed power-house and office workers into the plant, but Ford refused to talk while pickets remained. Binding arbitration was imposed and Mr. Justice Ivan C. Rand of the Supreme Court of Canada

began searching for a workable solution. He first chastized the union for its lawlessness, and Ford for its intransigence. Then he got down to business.

Rand rejected the notion of a closed union shop requiring everyone to join, but he agreed that workers benefitting from union activity should pay their share.

The historic Rand Formula remains today as one of Canada's most important pieces of labour jurisprudence. It stipulated compulsory dues, while not compelling people to join the union. It also decided that workers would be penalized financially if they participated in "wildcat" strikes and that the company would pay into pension and life insurance funds, as well as provide guaranteed minimum yearly employment and a minimum wage.

The strike was settled on December 19, representing an historic step in guaranteeing union security.

On Wednesday, January 2, 1946, 5,000 tired but jubilant workers were back on the job, welcoming the New Year and the end of the war — both overseas and at home.

Ford workers paralyzed much of Windsor's east end when they commandeered cars, trucks and buses to blockade Riverside Drive and nearby feeder streets.

The Changing Times

The Auto Pact Provided Freer Trade Movement Of Cars And Parts

The auto industry changed radically and historically in the 1960s after a one-man Royal Commission looked closely at the business, analyzing its direction and impact on Canadian workers.

Car makers were in a slump and unemployment was chronic in Windsor when Vincent W. Bladen, an economist at the University of Toronto, began his study.

Bladen's report made a number of important recommendations. He felt that car manufacturing in Canada and the U.S. should be seen as a single, integrated North American entity instead of two separate and distinct elements. Bladen also realized that taxes on cars coming into Canada were no higher than 14 per cent, yet Canadian taxes on cars produced in Canada totalled 18 per cent. That four-per-cent difference, combined with a higher Canadian dollar, meant that cars were actually more expensive in Canada.

Bladen recommended easing taxes and softening content requirements to encourage foreign investment. He also suggested (and this would be key) eliminating duties on parts and vehicles, as long as manufacturers increased Canadian production.

The idea was to balance import and export values. It was a form of free trade with Canadian parts and vehicles going to the U.S. in the same percentage as they were entering Canada.

On January 6, 1965, Canada and the U.S. signed a paper called the "Agreement Concerning Auto Products between the U.S. and Canada" — the Auto Pact. It was the first Canada-U.S. trade deal providing a degree of freer trade movement between American and Canadian branch plants. The Auto Pact helped to mould the two countries into one huge auto market. After the deal, some models built exclusively in one country could be sold throughout North America.

Detractors claim the deal created an economic recession and mass foreign car invasion. Canada suffered a trade deficit in each of the first three years of the 1970s. In 1979 the deficit climbed to an alarming $3 billion.

Meanwhile, the manufacture of parts shifted somewhat to the U.S. Some American companies acquired Canadian companies to meet the Canadian-made parts requirements. Overall it led to rationalization of auto plants and sparked the restructuring of the Canadian industry.

Ninety-five new plants were built in Canada and there were 169 expansions at existing plants including Chrysler and GM in Windsor.

Production of cars and trucks increased from 670,000 to more than 1,000,000. Twenty thousand more workers found jobs, and exports rose from 51,000 to more than 500,000. One industry analyst says that, for Canada, the Auto Pact was embarassingly successful.

On the down side, Canada still bought more cars than it sold, and some safety regulations went by the boards. If a rear window defroster wasn't required in the U.S., then there was no defroster.

Canadians also worked at unskilled production-line jobs, while research, design and development remained in the U.S. Corporate management was concentrated more heavily in Detroit, along with investment, purchasing, export and production decisions.

Part Five:
A City Like No Other

Someone once said, more in truth than in jest, that if it was Made in Canada, had four wheels and an engine, it was probably assembled, fabricated, moulded, cast, drilled, bored or painted in Windsor.

Over the past 90 years, Windsor has had a hand in building parts, or all, of millions of cars, trucks, buses and war machines.

Pound-for-pound, the skilled hands of Windsor have contributed more toward the Canadian economy than any other manufacturing centre in the country.

Boosters have promoted Windsor as The Banana Belt, City of Roses and Sun Parlour.

It is all of those things — but in the end, it remains the Automotive Capital of Canada.

PREVIOUS PAGE:

As the automotive industry matured, it was important to find more efficient ways of moving finished cars to market. Trains and boats provided the earliest forms of mass transportation. At one time, lumber frames were built to lock the cars into position. At the far left, the cars were driven onto three decks, increasing load capacity and speeding delivery to waiting customers.
Today, hydraulic lifts (top right) are frequently used to load truck carriers.
Photos: Carl Morgan collection, Chrysler Canada and François Baby House Museum.

Across Canada — And Through The Rockies

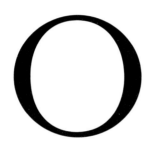

nce car makers got the hang of how to put a machine together, the next thing was to figure out how to capture public attention, sell it, and turn a profit.

They tried every gimmick from skidding recklessly across frozen lakes, to climbing craggy mountain slopes — or the steps of public buildings.

Many companies entered gruelling inter-continental car rallies to prove the durability of their products. They bumped along on rutted, dirt tracks and crossed fast-running rivers. These promotional odysseys, endurance tests for man and machine, were popular among adventurous salesmen who made their passionate pitches wherever people would listen in Small Town Canada.

One of the earliest entrepreneurial companies was Reo Motors of St. Catharines, which launched a cross-Canada tour on August 27, 1912. E. V. Haney and J. W. Wilby dipped the rear wheels of their car into the Atlantic and set off on a seven-week, 4,200-mile trek.

The drive-shaft broke, the tires burst, and they filled rutted roads with stones. When a new drive-shaft twisted, they limped along, covering 200 miles in five days. When the road ended, the two travelled 80 miles by boat to Sault Ste. Marie. They arrived in Winnipeg by train, built their own corduroy roads on the Prairies and pushed their car up steep slopes in the Rockies. Near Cranbrook, B.C., they were pulled out of a swamp by horses, and finally took a raft and train to Vancouver.

They delivered a letter from the mayor of Halifax and went on to Port Alberni on Vancouver Island. In triumph, Haney boasted that one tire still had "Halifax air".

FORD OF CANADA ARCHIVES

Ford engineers designed dignified vehicles for funeral needs.

The indomitable Charlie Speers, who became manager of Champion Spark Plug Company's Windsor office, poses in front of one of the sales trucks. Speers and co-worker Cal Evans drove from Windsor to Vancouver, becoming the first Canadians to cross the Rockies in a car.

Five years later, humourless pedestrians were still shouting "get a horse" as Charlie Speers and Cal Evans, representing Champion Spark Plug in Windsor, began a sales trip from Windsor to Vancouver — becoming the first motorists to cross the Rockies under their own power.

Speers became manager of Champion's Windsor office. In the early days, his job was to spread the good word about Champion sparkplugs. He had a panel truck fitted onto a Ford Chassis, covered it with advertising and was forever leaving on bone-jarring sales junkets.

The trip to Vancouver took all summer, with Speers and Evans stopping at every garage and hardware store to build a dealer network. Evans set up displays while Speers sold and explained how to clean sparkplugs.

Serious trouble developed while crossing the Prairies. There were few roads and they followed meandering wagon trails, hitting wide stretches where farmers had plowed, obliterating the path. They spent days searching for other tracks to follow.

In the Rockies, the road went only to Creston, B.C. Undaunted, Speers believed that only two trains went through each day and, as soon as one train passed, he drove onto the tracks, straddling one rail and bumping along the gravel-and-tie bed. What they hadn't counted on was a freight making an unscheduled run. They could hear the train and see the smoke as it puffed up a steep slope.

With a river on one side and a mountain wall on the other, there was no place to go until they reached a narrow fissure, opening into a dry ravine. Speers and Evans pried the car off the tracks and over the embankment moments before the train whistled past.

This 1926 Model T was the first car to cross Canada coast-to-coast. It was driven by Ed Flickenger, manager of Ford's photographic section, and Doctor Doolittle, president of the Canadian Automobile Association.

It took two days with a block-and-tackle to get back on track and resume the trip. When they arrived in Vancouver in October, 1917, they were greeted by a convoy of cars and escorted to City Hall for an official welcome.

Speers was just one of many "Champluggers". He travelled the world and became known as "Singapore Charlie".

• • •

On September 8, 1925 — to celebrate Ford's 21st birthday and demonstrate the need for a trans-Canada highway — Ford sent a 1926 Model "T" coast-to-coast. It was the first car to cross Canada under its own power.

The car was driven by Ed Flickenger, manager of Ford's photographic section in Windsor, and Doctor Doolittle, president of the Canadian Automobile Association. The trip took 40 rough-riding days and covered 4,794 miles. In the heavily-wooded Maritimes, Flickenger hacked a path wide enough for the car. On the Prairies they hit an 800-mile stretch where roads didn't exist, but mud flats did. In the Rockies they crawled along steep mountain passes. Unlike Speers, when the going got tough, Flickenger installed special flanged wheels, allowing him to run on the tracks.

He was listed as the Ford Special on the railway schedule, permitting him to ride the rails without fear of trains. His car had four tire punctures and needed one mechanical adjustment. He jacked the car up 14 times to change the wheels.

The historic trip was reversed in 1973 by two Mustangs and two Cougars, which ended up in St. John's, Newfoundland. The trek was billed as the "Return of Flickenger".

In 1992, Ford sent four Taurus sedans from Halifax to Vancouver using a variety of alternate fuels.

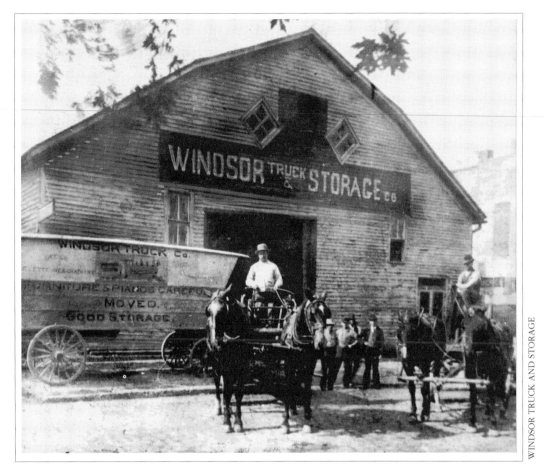

When Windsor Truck and Storage Company was founded, horses and covered wagons (above) were used to carry on business. The word "truck" was used then as a verb — as in trucking, or carrying goods. When the auto industry began producing commercial vehicles, WT&S moved with the times. The truck (right) and tractor-trailer (above right) were early additions.

Trucks And The Business World

If the advent of the personal automobile changed, forever, the social and domestic lives of the people who bought them, imagine what the transition from horse-drawn wagon to motorized trucks did for those who made their livings in the world of trade and commerce!

General truckers, movers, deliverymen, livery operators no longer had to face the dawn of each day with the dreary chore of feeding, watering and harnessing teams of horses before getting on with whatever tasks were in store for them.

Windsor Truck and Storage, founded in 1880 by Tim Foran, is Windsor's oldest trucking company and is still a leader in the field.

Lancaster Cartage started as a produce trucking business, with a single vehicle.

As Lancaster Cartage grew, so did its fleet of Model T trucks.

One of Windsor's largest trucking companies, founded by E. W. Lancaster, had its beginning as a modest fruit store in 1914-15. Edward Lancaster began with a single truck, picking up produce shipped by rail to Windsor, then delivering it to market. By 1929, the company expanded to furniture moving.

Roy Lancaster joined his father in 1947 and the company began hauling steel. During the 1950s and '60s, Lancaster Cartage and Hauling was one of the biggest customers of the Ambassador Bridge Company. That association led to Roy Lancaster joining the bridge company, and his eventual appointment as president.

The Teahan Furniture Company: Pile it on, tie it down, and move along.

Fred Bertrand Livery and Taxi Service in Amherstburg was one of the many rural companies to take advantage of the opportunities open to commercial enterprises by the expanding automotive industry. The company quickly retired its horse-drawn vehicles (below) in favour of a fleet of trucks (right).

Champion Spark Plug Company worker loads crates of sparkplugs into a light-duty Model T truck.

How many changes have we witnessed since the beginning of the automotive era?

Left: The electric refrigerator replaced the kitchen icebox, and the need for ice deliveries melted away.

Lower left: The 1925 LaFrance firetruck outlived its usefulness and was donated to the Historic Vehicle Society Museum on the Arner Town Line, where it is kept in operational condition.

Lower right:
Baum and Brody, one of Windsor's long-time downtown furniture dealers, depended on early stake trucks to make its deliveries, but the company closed its doors in 1977.

A City Like No Other

Ford

Though the town has virtually become known as Ford, when incorporated in June, 1912 as a village of some 850 population, it was called Ford City in the articles of incorporation, and again in 1915, when raised to the status of a town it was called Ford City in the Gazette. Now it is almost invariably called Ford, and Ford it will likely remain to be known by.

It need hardly be mentioned that the town received its name from the Canadian establishment of the Ford Motor Company. This corporation came to Ford City in 1904, and began manufacturing motor cars for Dominion and export trade. From that time on the plant has continued to grow, and officials state that the end of the company's expansion is not yet in sight. Although practically the "baby" of the Border Cities, the town has made great progress, and is modern in every particular. Street paving, sewer construction and water mains are being proceeded with as rapidly as possible. Land values have increased tremendously in the past few years, too, and still many home are being constructed.

It was on the site of the present town that the Ottawa Indians had their tribe village in the summer of 1763, the time of the Pontiac conspiracy. It was a rendezvous then of the great but treacherous Indian chief.

Riverside, the municipality adjoining Ford City on the east, was incorporated as a town in the spring of this year. It is a particularly splendid residential section with a decidedly progressive spirit.

CIVIC ADMINISTRATION

Mayor—E. C. Poisson
Town Engineer—W. H. Patterson
Town Assessor—Joseph L. Reaume
Town Clerk—J. F. Foster
Treasurer—J. F. Foster
Solicitors—Furlong, Furlong and Co.
Magistrate—W. E. Gundy
Tax Collector—Joseph La Pierre
Chief of Police—A. Maisonville
Fire Chief—A. Maisonville.
Meets Tuesdays in Town Hall, Sandwich street, Ford.

TOWN COUNCIL, 1921

Meets Tuesdays in Town Hall, Sandwich street, Ford, on Tuesdays, at 8.00 p.m., Eastern Standard Time.

Mayor

E. C. Poisson

A "City" In Name Alone

Today, the names of Ford City and East Windsor are little more than a faint memory in the minds of a few people — yet, for many years, they were the hub of the Canadian car industry.

Ford City, which never gained city status, was incorporated as a village in 1913, became East Windsor in 1929, and was amalgamated by the City of Windsor in 1935.

*N.B.— The date of 1912 shown in the classified directory at left is an error. It should read 1913.

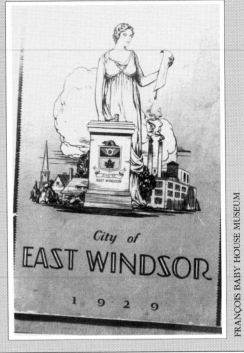

City of
EAST WINDSOR
1 9 2 9

The East Windsor Fire Station was on Drouillard Road near Riverside Drive. The vehicles in this photo are a 1924 LaFrance ladder truck, 1922 LaFrance pumper and a Model T Ford.

HOWARD WATTS COLLECTION

Ford City never was a "city", but it was certainly not a backwater community, judging by the substantial post office building (below) and the town hall (left). Although the municipality was incorporated as "Ford City", it was most often referred to as "Ford". Even the post office managed to carry Ford's winged emblem over the door. The street car's destination is also shown as "Ford".

FORD OF CANADA ARCHIVES

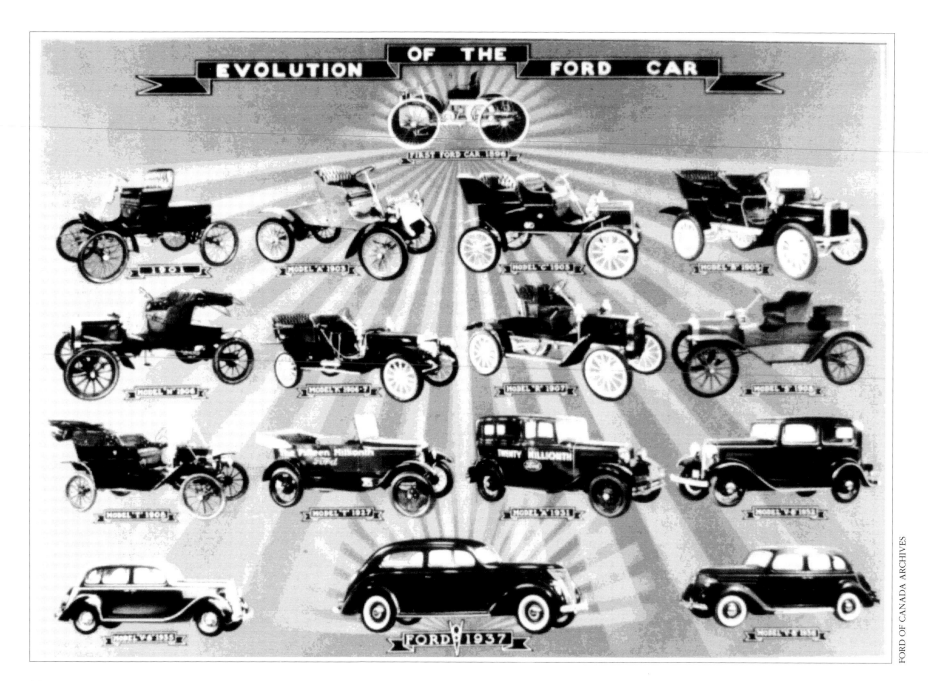

The evolution of the Ford motor car from its inception until 1937.

When Prime Minister Sir Wilfrid Laurier visited Windsor on September 9, 1911, he was greeted at the Grand Trunk Railway Station by a number of civic dignitaries including Gordon McGregor, founder of the Ford Motor Company of Canada, shown at the wheel of the car. Beside Mr. McGregor is Hon. W. C. Kennedy, later to become minister of railways. In the rear seat is Sir Wilfrid (hand on cane) and Rt. Hon. George P. Graham.

Windsor classic car collector Nick Romanick sits proudly behind the wheel of a 1931 Madame X Imperial Limousine. It is one of two 15-cylinder Cadillacs built in Detroit. The second Imperial was owned by Sam McLaughlin, the late president of General Motors of Canada. The McLaughlin car had a silver inlay stripe on the side and gold-plated interior door handles.

In 1740, Sergeant Louis Villaire dit St. Louis, a French soldier serving in Detroit, took up a land grant in the Turkey Creek area. Over the years, some of his descendants settled in what is now the St. Rose area of the former town of Riverside. Their farm fronted on the Detroit River and ran east to Isabelle Place.

It's perhaps fitting that they were also pioneers in the infant years of the auto age. Alphonse St. Louis and his brother, Alfred, found a variety of uses for an early motorcycle with side-car. They used it to carry packages (left) or to simply move around the farm more quickly (below).

Millions and millions of cars, trucks, buses, fire engines and military machines have rolled off Windsor assembly lines since 1904. Traditionally, milestones are marked with in-plant ceremonies. In this instance, Chrysler Canada celebrated the arrival of the one millionth minivan — less than four years after the Windsor Assembly Plant went into production. October, 1993 marked the 10th anniversary and, as the year drew to a close, minivan production approached 3,000,000.

Epilogue

Throughout the first half of the 20th Century, Windsor was Car Maker to the Nation.

The city grew up making cars, trucks and war machines by the millions. As auto assembly plants came and went, parts-makers, tool-and-die and mold-making companies followed. They shared in the feasts — and the famines.

With freer trade, tougher overseas competition, changing buyer habits, and a tighter economy, the industry survived a dramatic evolution — as did Windsor.

Except for Chrysler, car assembly diminished while the parts industry grew, moving to Centre Stage. Windsor emerged as a major source of engines, transmissions and door panels. It also earned a reputation as a leader in tool-and-die and machine tooling, especially injection and plastic molding.

The year 1993 was one of turmoil for the Big Three. The name of the game was "survival" as the Big Three continued belt-tightening, trimming staff and changing senior manage-

ment. The big-buck decision-making part of the business has always been gut-wrenching as corporations struggle for that thin, but crucial, competitive edge.

The end of the movement toward "lean and mean" management is not in sight, and industry observers predict the shakeout will continue until the end of the century. Even the aggressive Japanese faced challenges from Korea, Vietnam and Eastern Europe, struggling to hold their ground. Today, there are three major North American manufacturers, nine in Japan and eight in Europe — all playing a game of musical chairs. Some won't make it — and those that do will be vastly different than they were in 1993.

• • •

The industrial map has changed dramatically in the 90 years since Henry Ford met Gordon McGregor. Billions have been spent relocating assembly plants throughout Ontario. Some car makers are already in Mexico, others are tempted by low

Considering the impact of global competition on the entire auto industry, manufacturers constantly search for ways to cut costs. One transitional step was for electric robot welders (above) to replace workers garbed in uniforms that resembled space suits (below).

wages and softer labour and pollution control laws.

Clare Winterbottom is with Anchor Lamina, which makes die sets for the auto industry, a supplier to the tool-and-die and mold industries. He's satisfied with the industrial climate in Ontario and, while he'll sell to Mexico, he has no plans to move. His sales were up 23 per cent in 1993 over 1992.

Mold maker Joe Ouellette of Acrolab Instruments Limited echoes those sentiments. He says there are 50 different mold-making shops in Windsor and Essex County, each averaging $5 million worth of work. A hundred more companies supply them.

Ouellette says that 10 years ago, his furthest customer was 100 miles away. Now he's dealing with China, Russia, Germany, Japan, Korea and France. Location and proximity to markets are no longer serious factors if you're good at what you do.

• • •

The auto industry has always been on the sharp edge of technological change, finding new, inexpensive and creative ways to use machines, computers and robots.

The latest buzz-word is "rapid-prototyping", where designers use computers to guide a machine to make a part in a day instead of weeks. Computers cut, bore and drill metal flawlessly and repeatedly.

In a very real sense, history is repeating itself. We're in the midst of a new Industrial Revolution.

At the turn of the last century, we shifted from an age of skilled craftsmen who produced everything by hand, to an age of mass production with interchangeable parts and cookie-cutter simplicity. Now, robots move in eerie silence, tirelessly and with precision, welding and spray painting faster and easier without sacrificing quality. The human role has been reduced to monitoring.

• • •

If there's one thing clear as we move from the 20th to the 21st Century, the only constant is change. The only guarantee of stability is the industry's willingness to adapt. Anyone

A search of The Windsor Star library's historical photo files turned up this compelling and appealing picture of a group of men, identified only as a group of "Ford workers". The picture was apparently taken about 1904 to 1906. While it is likely the setting was McGregor's Walkerville Ford factory, that assumption could not be confirmed.

expecting more is not in touch with reality.

Walter M. P. McCall, Chrysler Canada's manager of corporate public relations, says that, for competitive reasons, car companies can only talk about the future in broad terms. He predicts there won't be a tremendous difference in the way cars look but there will be greater emphasis on aerodynamics. Changes for the sake of appearance will take a back seat to quality and dependability. Cars mustn't break down, but if they do, they should be cheap and easy to fix.

There will be fewer parts. More plastic and aluminum, heat-resistant ceramics and synthetics will reduce weight and improve fuel economy. Already, all-aluminum bodies are proposed for Ford Taurus and Mercury Sable. Chrysler is using stainless steel exhausts. Micro-chips will replace even more components under the hood. Chrysler is banking on its new "cab forward" concept, where the windshield and cowl have been moved forward to create a larger, more comfortable passenger compartment. The interior will look more like a living room with picture windows.

There will be more computer gadgets, and dashboards may even include an electronic navigation system, complete with maps offering alternative routes to avoid traffic jams. Mayday transmitters could send distress calls.

Selective cruise control may move the car in relation to the speed of traffic. Collision-avoidance systems could include automatic braking.

Detroit's 1992 International Auto Show indicated that gimmicks were out, dependability, safety and environmental

Think of it: Ford's five-passenger Touring Car (left) and Chrysler's Dodge Van (above) were built roughly 80 years apart, to serve much the same purpose — provide comfortable transportation for the travelling family. Oh, yes, aside from the obvious design differences, the price for the Windsor-built Ford was listed at $530.

concerns are in. Air-bags, anti-lock brakes, CFC-free air conditioners and recyclable plastic parts were spotlighted. Look for cars with recycled pop bottles in the roof upholstery, reclaimed bumpers, interior trim and instrument panels as sound-deadening material, mud flaps and grille parts.

The industry is also developing city-only vehicles with removable doors as well as battery, electric or solar-powered systems. Sloping windows could provide warmth in winter, and heat deflectors cool comfort in summer.

Manufacturers remain nervous about more government legislation aimed at 40 miles to the gallon, better child protective seats and other passenger safety devices, all of which will add to the sticker price. McCall, a 20-year veteran in the business, says cost is a big concern, but companies will learn to cope — or they won't survive.

• • •

Much has changed since the '50s and '60s. When hype surrounded the release of new models, and tight security prevented the public from learning what was under wraps until the magic hour.

The element of surprise was an important part of the marketing strategy, but the days are gone when consumers bought whatever the company showcased. Manufacturers must tailor their cars to a specific market — luxurious looks that are easy on the pocketbook.

Styling, however, is a two-edged sword. Designers must anticipate public tastes — but can't race ahead. The industry paid dearly for those lessons with the release of Ford's Edsel and the Chrysler Airflow. Both bombed when they hit the marketplace.

It takes three years and billions of dollars to introduce a new model. Failures can't be bankrolled any more.

• • •

Each new economic downturn sparks fresh chatter about

the need to "diversify" and avoid the humps and hollows that bedevil what is essentially a one-industry city.

The problem is that bringing new industry to town can't be legislated. An active Industrial Development Commission works aggressively to "sell" Windsor as an ideal place to locate and has gained ground over the years.

Beyond that, new industries come or they don't — depending on what their own market studies tell them about their needs.

•••

The question remains: What does the future hold?

Free trade between Canada, the U.S. and Mexico, signed in 1993, included strengthening of the Auto Pact. North American content regulations were increased to 62 per cent from 50 for cars, trucks and engines. Tariffs and other production restrictions were removed. The new rules also applied to Mexico, allowing companies to capitalize on cheaper Mexican labour.

Despite those assurances, unions felt the pact was being eroded. The new deal prompted union and North American manufacturers to push for an extension of the agreement to include Japan and Korea. Those countries were establishing plants in Canada, increasing their level of imports and decreasing Canada's share of the parts production market.

How Windsor will fare in the end is anybody's guess. It's a business in which anything can happen — and probably will.

•••

Cars are Big News everywhere, especially in this sliver of Southwestern Ontario where, at times, the fascination for the automobile colours everything else.

Windsor is a factory town, a union town with a working class innocence. Almost a century of Windsor families have lived in the long shadow of the Big Three, within sight of a tool shop, or earshot of a stamping plant. The auto industry permeates the very fabric of the city.

In what is almost a throw-back to the 1950s and '60s, balmy spring and summer evenings are still given over to one of the youthful rites of passage — cruising the Main Drag.

On Friday and Saturday nights, before police throw up "Emergency Vehicles Only" barricades, the throbbing of ghetto blasters mixes with the relentless roar of engines, the blare of honking horns. High-pitched shouts and whistles bounce off the walls as the cars thread their way to The River, pause to pay homage to the monolithic Detroit skyline, turn, and head back again.

There's a fascination for the automobile in Windsor that transcends the fact that the city manufactures cars and car parts. The automobile is a proud statement of individuality. Each generation has its own fad, from fin and chrome of the '50s to spoilers, racing stripes, mag wheels and sun roof. They're as much a part of the allure as the ornament dangling from the rearview mirror, the bumper sticker and personalized licence plate.

There's a passion, power, sexual potency, ego-tripping, self-importance, feel-rich, and feel-good sense of self-identification to the automobile. It's a heady combination, part of the psyche of Windsor. They are the feelings that keep the industry young, vibrant, thriving — and absolutely essential to a self-indulgent society.

As one century draws to a close and we prepare to enter another, there are no sure bets, but the odds are that Windsor will continue to play an ever-changing, but key role, as Car Maker to a Nation.

Sources

BOOKS:

BAILEY, L. Scott. "GM. The First 75 Years of Transportation Products." Detroit, Michigan: Editors of Automobile Quarterly Magazine, 1983.

BARLOW, R. T. "A Capsule History of The Automotive Industry in Windsor, Essex County and Chatham." Windsor Public Library. 1986.

BIRD, Anthony. "Antique Automobiles." London: Treasure Press, 1967.

BOTSFORD, David P. C.M. "At The End of The Trail". Amherstburg: Eds. Eleanor Gignac and Effie Botsford, 1985.

CANNON, William A. and FOX, Fred K. "Studebaker: The Complete Story." Blue Ridge Summit P.A.: Modern Automotive Series. Tab Books Inc, 1981.

CHAUVIN, Francis X. M.D. "Men of Achievement: Essex County." Windsor: Volume One, 1927; Volume Two, 1929.

COLLIER, Peter and HOROWITZ, David. "The Fords: An American Epic." New York, N.Y. Summit Books, 1987.

COLLINS, Robert. "A Great Way to Go: The Auto in Canada." Toronto: Ryerson Press, 1969.

DeBONDT, John. "Canada on Wheels: A Portfolio of Early American Cars." Canada: Oberon Press. 1970.

DeBONDT, John. "They Don't Make 'Em Like That Any More. A Picture History of Canadian Cars 1932 -47." Canada: Oberon Press. 1987.

DURNFORD, Hugh and BAECHLER, Glenn. "Cars of Canada: A Craven Foundation History." Toronto: McClelland and Stewart, 1973.

DYKES, James. "Canada's Automotive Industry: Canada at Work Series." Toronto: McGraw Hill Company of Canada Limited, 1970.

FORD MOTOR COMPANY OF CANADA, LIMITED. "Military Vehicles." Windsor: Ford Motor Company.

FORD MOTOR COMPANY OF CANADA, LIMITED. "Ford of Canada in Wartime: A Record of Wartime Advertising in Canadian Newspapers, Magazines and Periodicals 1941-45." Windsor: Ford Motor Company. 1946.

FORD MOTOR COMPANY OF CANADA, LIMITED. "Ford at Fifty: An American Story." New York: Simon and Schuster Inc. 1953.

GERVAIS, C.H. "The Border Police: 125 Years of Policing in Windsor." Waterloo: Penumbra Press 1992.

GREGG, William A. "Canada's Fighting Vehicles: Europe 1943-45. Canadian Military Vehicle Series Volume One." Rockwood: Canadian Military Historical Society Incorporated, 1979.

GREGG, William A. "Canadian Military Vehicles Profile. Canadian Military Vehicle Series Volume Two." Rockwood: Canadian Military Historical Society Incorporated, 1979.

GREGG, William A. "Blueprint for Victory: The Story of Military Vehicle Design and Production in Canada, 1937-45. Canadian Military Vehicle Series Volume Three." Rockwood: Canadian Military Historical Society Incorporated, 1979.

IACOCCA, Lee and NOVAK, William. "Iacocca: An Autobiography." Toronto: Bantam Books, 1984.

JACOBS, Timothy. "Lemons: The World's Worst Cars." London: Brian Brooks Ltd. 1991.

KULISEK, Larry and PRICE, Trevor. "Windsor 1892-1992 A Centennial Celebration Illustrated History" Windsor: Chamber Publications. 1992.

MAY, George S. "R.E. Olds: Auto Industry Pioneer." Grand Rapids, Michigan: William B. Eerdman's Publishing Company. 1977.

MONTAGU, Lord of Beaulieu and McCOMB, Wilson F. "Behind the Wheel: The Magic and Manners of Early Motoring." New York and London: Paddington Press Ltd. 1977.

MORRISON, Neil F. "Garden Gateway to Canada: 100 Years of Windsor and Essex County 1854-1954." Toronto: Ryerson Press, 1954.

NEVINS, Allen. "Ford: The Times, The Man, The Company." New York. Charles Scribner's and Sons 1954.

PERRY, Ross. "The Future of Canada's Auto Industry, The Big Three and The Japanese Challenge." Ottawa: The Canadian Institute for Economic Policy, 1982.

SEDGWICK, Michael. "Classic Car Guide: Antique Cars." Canada: John Wiley and Sons Ltd. 1980.

SEDGWICK, Michael. "Early Cars: Pleasures and Treasures." London: Weidenfeld and Nicolson, 1962.

SEIFFERT, Ulrich and WALZER, Peter. "Auto Technology of the Future." Warrendale, P.A.: Society of Automotive Engineers, 1991.

WHITE, Bob. "Hard Bargains. My Life On The Line." Toronto: McClelland and Stewart, 1987.

ZAVITZ, Perry R. "Canadian Cars 1946-1984." Baltimore, Maryland: Bookman Publishing, 1985.

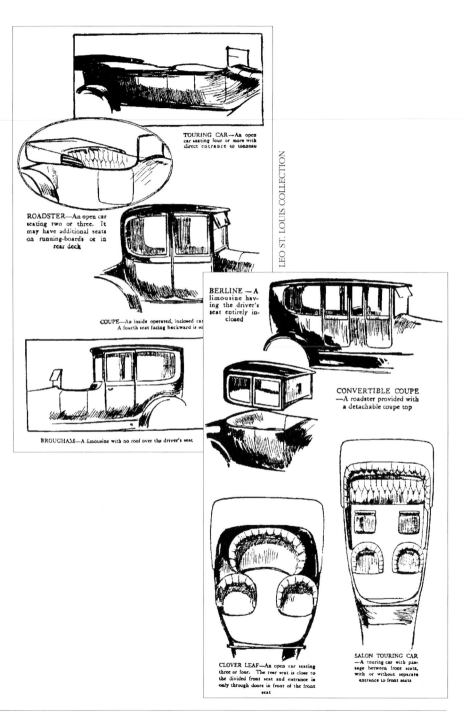

PERIODICALS:

AMHERSTBURG PUBLIC LIBRARY. "Index of Amherstburg Industries." Excerpts from Amherstburg Echo and The Windsor Daily Star.

BOWMAN, H. Wieand, GOTTLIEB, Robert J. "Classic Cars and Antiques" Magazine. Los Angeles, California: Motor Trend Books Inc., 1953.

BOWMAN, H. Wieand. "Famous Old Cars: An Album of Automobile Classics." Magazine. Greenwich, Connecticut: Fawcett Publications, 1957.

CBC RADIO 1550. "Radio Noon Archives."

Interview: Kimberley Juras, Georgia Klym-Skeates, Curator, Southwestern Ontario Heritage Village. Kingsville, August 4, 1992.

Interview: Herb Colling/Jim Scratch, Car Collector, Windsor, September 1992.

"Morning Watch Archives."

Interview: Tom Aubin, Ford Plant and Car Show Stories. Windsor and Detroit, January, 1993.

CBC TV, VISUAL IMAGE PRODUCTIONS. "Ploughshares Into Swords. The Militia in Essex County." TV Documentary, Windsor.

CHRYSLER CANADA. Archives and Photo Collection. Windsor Chrysler Canada Headquarters. 1992.

DROUILLARD, Bernard W. "Transit In Windsor." Transit Windsor.

ESSEX COUNTY HISTORICAL ASSOCIATION. "Radio Sketches 1963." Essex Public Library.

FISHER BODY INC. "Fisher Body Craftsman 75th Anniversary Edition, 1983." Warren, Mich. Ed. Jim Sponseller, 1983.

FORD MOTOR COMPANY. "Ford Graphic." Windsor: Associated Editors. Alec McAlister and Ernest Todd. 1950.

"Annual Report: Golden Jubilee Year, 1904-1954." Windsor. 1954.

"Backfire." Ford Propaganda Film. Montreal: Assoc. Screen Studios, Courtesy CBC-TV, ca 1940s.

"Ford Times." Windsor: 1914-1917.

FREEMAN, C.M. "Grandson of Canada: Walter P. Chrysler." MacLean's Magazine. March 15, 1933.

GENERAL MOTORS. "GM War Craftsman." Magazine. Oshawa: Ed. Geo. A. Fletcher, 1943-1945.

GM TRIM PLANT. "15th Anniversary Special Edition." Windsor, 1980.

HIPPENSTEELE, Lee B. "Thirty Years with Walter P. Chrysler." Hershey, Pennsylvania: Antique Automobile Club of America, May 1962.

HISTORICAL VEHICLE SOCIETY OF ONTARIO. "Through the Windshield." Newsletters. Windsor Public Library, 1970-1985.

HUTTON, Eric, McLAUGHLIN, R.S. "My Eighty Years on Wheels." Macleans. Sept. 15, Oct. 1, Oct. 15, 1954.

McCALL, Walter, M.P. "The Society of Automotive Historians. Henry M. Leland Chapter: Tour of Border City Automotive Historic Sites." Windsor, April 10, 1984.

McCALL, Walter, M.P. "The Chrysler Story". Car Guide Magazine. Fall, 1992.

NATIONAL ASSOCIATION OF ANTIQUE AUTO CLUBS OF CANADA. "Vintage Canada". Toronto. Craven Foundation, 1974.

PACKARD. "Inner Circle. Vol 16, Number 15". Detroit, Michigan, 1931.

SMITH, Herman L. "Model 'T' Dominated Roads." Article. Windsor: Windsor Public Library/Ford of Canada.

UAW SOLIDARITY. "UAW: Forty Years of Struggle, A Special UAW History Issue." Detroit, Michigan. 1977.

WINDSOR EVENING RECORD, BORDER CITIES STAR, THE WINDSOR STAR. "Automotive Articles." Windsor, 1902-present.

WINDSOR PUBLIC LIBRARY. "Windsor and Essex County Historical Scrapbooks." Volumes 2, 3D, 9, 14D, 15, 15A, 15B, 62.

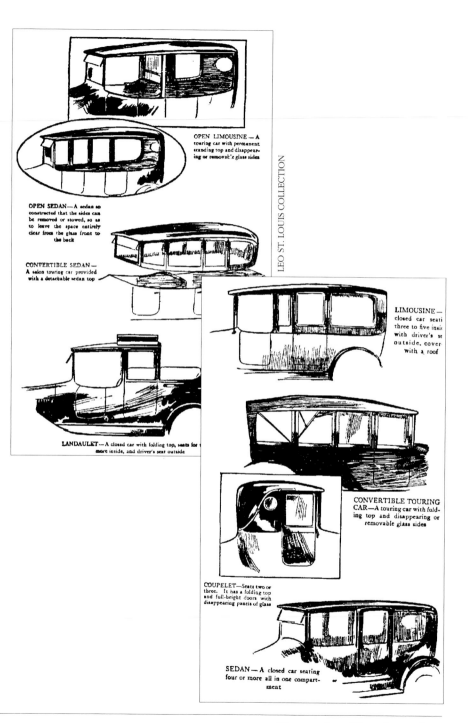